THE
OBJECT OF
MORAL PHILOSOPHY
ACCORDING TO
ST. THOMAS AQUINAS

Richard P. Geraghty, S.M., Ph.D.

Sinclair Community College
Dayton, Ohio

UNIVERSITY
PRESS OF
AMERICA

ISBN (Perfect): 0-8191-2162-2
ISBN   (Cloth): 0-8191-2161-4

Library of Congress Number: 81-40713

To My Fellow Brothers

Acknowledgement of permission to reprint excerpts from the following work:

Jacques Maritain, <u>The Degrees of Knowledge</u>. Translated from the fourth French edition under the supervision of Gerald B. Phelan. Copyright © 1959 by Jacques Maritain. Reprinted with the permission of Charles Scribner's Sons.

I would also like to acknowledge my debt to Barbara Kramer and Josept Zeinz, S.M., who so greatly helped in the preparation of the manuscript; to the professors in Toronto, especially one, who taught me; and finally to the Marianists, who supported me lo these many years.

R. P. G.

TABLE OF CONTENTS

FOREWORD

A topic discussed in a recent (September, 1981) Symposium at the University of Calgary was the difference between philosophy and ideology. Very confidently a couple of papers drew the distinction from an alleged contrast between the objectives of the two ways of thinking. Philosophy limits itself to knowing. It is not concerned with doing anything. It consists in thought for the sake of thought only. When thought is put to use for directing action and life, you have ideology and no longer philosophy.

This estimate of the distinction straightway sounds shocking to ears accustomed to the Aristotelian description of practical philosophy. While theoretical philosophy bears essentially though not exclusively on knowledge for its own sake, practical philosophy aims essentially at turning out good persons and good citizens even when it is using theoretical knowledge. Its objective is good conduct. Accordingly in the Aristotelian tradition philosophy cannot be confined within the limits of the theoretical order. When operative in the practical realm, however, it exhibits a flexible procedure that does not permit reduction to the rigid lines of any theoretical cast, for its starting points are then located not in human ideas but in the individual actions of properly habituated human agents.

The ideological context, though, is far from being the only area in which philosophical procedure has in one way or another been restricted to the theoretical plane. Complaints that Thomistic moral thinking has in recent times been too theoretical are frequent. Nevertheless the ground for these complaints has not been investigated in depth. Everywhere there seems to be a palpable revulsion against making moral philosophy bear directly upon human action in the real world, apparently out of fear that the procedure would thereby lose its scientific and objective character. Very little if any serious attention has been paid to Aristotle's (E.N. VII,3,1147a26-28) assertion that while the conclusion of theoretical reasoning is affirmation, the immediate result of practical reasoning is action. Where the starting points are found in the real habituation of individuals, the conclusions correspondingly appear in real action. In that way the method of moral philosophy differs radically from theoretical procedure. Yet who among recent Thomistic writers has carried this conception of moral thinking back to its Aristotelian roots? Why has the radical difference from theoretical philosophy been so consistently missed? Surely investigation and explanation are required.

In his book <u>The Object of Moral Philosophy according to St. Thomas Aquinas</u>, Richard Geraghty accepts this thorny challenge. The book has been developed from his doctoral thesis on the topic in the University of Toronto. It examines the currently accepted procedures in Thomistic moral thinking and compares them with the texts of Aquinas himself. The results may be quite astonishing to readers who have been inclined to rest cosily in the various Neoscholastic approaches to ethics. Nevertheless anyone who likes to indulge in the complaint that Thomistic ethics in recent times has been too theoretical should be keenly interested in tracing the discontent back to the roots meant to provide moral philosophy with its life-giving nutriment. To recommend a book that undertakes this task is a genuine pleasure.

Joseph Owens, C.Ss.R.

October 8, 1981

CHAPTER I

THE PROBLEM CONCERNING THE OBJECT OF MORAL PHILOSOPHY AMONG THREE THOMISTIC COMMENTATORS

The aim of this book is to answer the question: what is the object[1] of moral philosophy[2] according to St. Thomas Aquinas. This question is the first and most important one that can be asked about moral science. For Thomas holds, as will become clear in the course of this book, that the nature (either speculative or practical) and method (either analytic or synthetic) of any science is ultimately determined by the object which specifies it.

Does such a basic question, however, need to be asked today? It does. In his books Les degres du savoir (1932)[3] and Science et sagesse (1935)[4] Jacques Maritain advanced views about the nature of moral science which initiated much debate among the Thomistic scholars. While authors such as Yves Simon[5] supported Maritain, others such as Th. Deman,[6] J.M. Ramirez[7] and Odon Lottin opposed him. In 1946 and again in 1954 Lottin[8] reviewed the state of the question before

---

[1]What is here called the object of moral philosophy is also known as its subject. Both terms designate what the science is about. More will be said about them in the due course of the argument.

[2]For St. Thomas moral philosophy may also be called moral science or ethics.

[3]J. Maritain, Distinguer pour unir ou les degrés du savoir, (Paris, 1932).

[4]J. Maritain, Science et sagesse, suivi d'éclaircissements sur la philosophie morale, (Paris, 1935).

[5]Yves Simon, Critique de la connaissance morale, (Paris, 1934).

[6]Th. Deman, "Sur l'organisation du savoir moral," Revue des philos. et theol., XXIII (1934), 258-269.

[7]J.M. Ramirez, "La science morale pratique," Bulletin thomiste, 4 (1934-36), 423-432.

[8]Odon Lottin, Principes de morale, vol. I, (Louvain, 1946), pp. 13-59. Lottin also expresses substantially the same views in the introduction to his book Morale fondamentale, vol. I, (Turin, 1954).

advancing his own views. The debate between Lottin and Maritain has not been taken up by anyone else. But books by William A. Wallace[9] and John Naus[10] have continued to investigate the practical nature of moral science. Furthermore, such authors as Vernon Bourke, Henri Renard, Austin Fagothey and John Oesterle have discussed the practical nature of moral science in the introductions to their textbooks.[11] But even a cursory review of all of these works would show that Thomists are far from unanimous in their opinions.

How can the great variety of opinion among the scholars be accounted for? A quick review of Lottin's introduction to his book Principes de morale reveals the source of the difficulties. Lottin begins by citing Aristotle, who states that speculative science has for its goal the knowledge of truth while practical science has for its goal action.[12] Lottin then refers to Aristotle's Nicomachean Ethics in which moral science is defined as practical. The implication is, quite correctly, that Aristotle defines the practical nature of moral science in the light of a twofold distinction between speculative and practical science in general.

Turning to St. Thomas, Lottin then declares: "The essentially practical nature of moral science has not escaped St. Thomas. One need only look over his commentary on the Ethics of Aristotle."[13] The commentary shows that Thomas at the very beginning of the work distinguishes between the objects of speculative and of practical science before defining the object of morals.

So far there does not seem to be any particular difficulty. It would seem that if one wishes to understand more about the practical nature of moral science,

---

[9] William A. Wallace, The Role of Demonstration in Moral Theology, (Washington, 1962).

[10] John Naus, The Nature of the Practical Intellect According to St. Thomas Aquinas, (Rome, 1959).

[11] These textbooks are listed in the bibliography.

[12] Lottin, Principes de morale, p. 13. "La science spéculative, écrit le Stagirite, a pour fin la connaissance du vrai, la science pratique a pour but l'action."

[13] Ibid., p. 14. "La nature essentiellement pratique de la science morale n'a pas dávantage échappé à saint Thomas a'Aquin. Il suffit à cet effet de parcourir son Commentaire sur l'Éthique d'Aristote."

one would look more deeply into the commentary on the
Ethics. Yet Lottin's discussion does not take this
turn. He asks:

> But what exactly is a practical science?
> In several texts concerning another subject,
> namely, the knowledge that God has of things,
> St. Thomas applies himself to delineating
> the outline of practical science. St. Thomas
> points out a threefold division of knowledge:
> a purely speculative knowledge, a purely
> practical knowledge, and a knowledge
> theoretical in part and practical in part
> (S.T. I, 14,16).[14]

Here Lottin mentions other texts in St. Thomas
which speak of a threefold division of knowledge.
While these texts do not refer directly to moral science, they do refer to practical science in the theological setting of God's productive knowledge of his
creatures. Why should these texts pose a problem
about the nature of practical science? Though Lottin
does not say so explicitly, the problem is this. If
there is a purely speculative knowledge, a partly speculative and a partly practical knowledge, and a purely
practical knowledge, then in which category is practical science to be found? It will not be found,
obviously, in the category of purely speculative
knowledge. Will it be found, then, in the category
of the partly speculative and the partly practical?
Or will it be found in the category of the purely
practical? How one answers this question about the
nature of practical science in general determines how
one defines one of the practical sciences, moral
philosophy.

The answer to the problem lies obviously in examining the texts in question.[15] At the end of his

---

[14]Ibid., p. 15. "Mais qu'est exactement une science pratique? En plusieurs textes relatifs à un autre
sujet, à savoir la connaissance que Dieu a des choses,
saint Thomas s'est appliqué à définir les contours de
la science pratique. Le saint Docteur distingue une
triple connaissance: une connaissance purement théorique, une connaissance purement pratique, et une connaissance en partie théorique et en partie pratique."

[15]The texts are: S.T. I, 14, 16; De Ver. 2,8;3,3.

examination, however, Lottin concludes: "As one can see, the terminology is not rigidly fixed; and unfortunately St. Thomas has nowhere applied these notions to moral science. The problem then remains open. . . ."[16]

As will be shown later, Lottin is correct in saying that the terminology of the texts is flexible. He is also correct in saying that Thomas does not explicitly apply the distinctions he has made regarding practical science to moral science. But is he correct in saying that Thomas has left the question open? Obviously, Lottin thinks that he is correct and so proceeds to examine the views of John of St. Thomas (1589-1644) and of Maritain before drawing his own conclusions.

The argument of this chapter will be that St. Thomas has not really left the question open. To support this contention section I of this chapter will initiate a preliminary investigation into two texts dealing explicitly with the definition of moral science itself. The conclusion will be that Thomas defines moral science in the light of a radical distinction between the speculative and the practical. Moral science, therefore, is to be found in the category of purely practical knowledge.

Section II will then present the reader with a typical text speaking of the threefold division of knowledge. Section III will show how each of the three commentators--Lottin, John of St. Thomas and Maritain--agree with each in defining moral science, not in the light of the radical twofold distinction, but in the light of the threefold division of knowledge. Thus moral science is found to be in the category of the partly speculative and the partly practical. The commentators, however, differ with each other about the precise nature of this knowledge. Lottin calls it both speculative _and_ practical. John of St. Thomas considers it to be speculative. And Maritain holds it to be speculatively practical. None of the commentators holds that moral science is purely or simply practical.

Section IV will draw the conclusion that the three

---

[16]_Ibid_., p. 16. "On le voit, la terminologie n'est pas strictement fixée; et malheureusement saint Thomas n'applique nulle part ces notions à la science morale. Le problème reste donc ouvert. . . ."

commentators seem to differ with St. Thomas' conception of moral science.

One note on the structure of the book's argument: the first two chapters are but a preparation for the detailed analysis of the introductory sections of Thomas' commentary on the Nicomachean Ethics of Aristotle, which takes place in chapters three, four and five. This preparation is necessary because the commentators, particularly John of St. Thomas and Maritain, have been so influential in the formation of modern Thomists that to read St. Thomas is almost to read him through their eyes. To review the opinions of these commentators, then, is much like reviewing one's own presuppositions about moral philosophy. It is the view of the author that many of these presuppositions interfere with a proper understanding of the text of St. Thomas.

I.   The Radical Distinction Between the Sciences

In his commentary on the Ethics[17] Thomas devotes the first fifty-four lines (as found in the new edition) to defining the object of moral philosophy. While we will examine this text in detail in chapter three, we will give a brief overview now. In this way the reader will be presented with the heart of the whole argument.

Thomas designates four orders of reality which relate to four kinds of reason's activity (I,1,14-24).[18] The first is the order which reason does not establish but only considers (ordo quem ratio non facit, sed solum considerat). The example given is the things of nature. The other three orders are things which reason establishes by its considerations (quem ratio considerando facit). These orders are first, that which reason establishes among its own mental acts. Since this order specifies the science of rational philosophy

---

[17]St. Thomas Aquinas, Sententia Libri Ethicorum, ed. R.A. Gauthier, in Opera Omnia, Leonine Edition, vols. 47½ and 47 (Rome, 1969). All references to this work will appear in the body of the text. For example, Book I, Chapter 2, lines 20-23 will appear as (I,2,20-23). All translations of this work will be mine.

[18]The full text and translation may be found below in chapter three, p. 54.

(logic), problems about its classification will not concern us. Then there is the order which reason establishes among the operations of the will and finally the order established among productive operations like building a house.

The contrast between the two general functions of reason in the face of reality (either non-operables or operables) indicates that the four specific orders may be reduced to two generic orders. The first is whatever is only contemplated by man. On the basis of this description, one may conclude that before this order man stands simply as a knower, a spectator. Consequently, his reason here is ruled or measured by the things it contemplates. The second order, however, is whatever is established by man. These are operations or their products. On the basis of this description, one may conclude that, because man is the cause of the realities in question, he is not ruled or measured by them. Rather he is their rule and measure.

Having shown that two generic orders of reality specify two distinct exercises of reason, Thomas then states: "Because the considerations of reason are perfected by the habit of science, the different sciences are determined according to the different orders which each properly considers. . . ."[19] Among the sciences specified by the first order are metaphysics and natural philosophy, both speculative sciences. Among the sciences specified by the second order are the practical sciences of moral philosophy and of the mechanical arts.

Thomas then defines a specific science within the generic habitus of the practical: ". . . the subject (subiectum) of moral philosophy is human operations as directed to a goal . . ." (I,1,52-54).

Later Thomas states a major consequence of the fact that moral science is practical. He describes the method of moral science as synthetic (modo compositivo) in contrast to the method of speculative science, which is analytic (modo resolutivo) (I,3,54-58).

---

[19]"Et quia consideratio rationis per habitum scientia perficitur, secundum hos diversos ordines quos proprie ratio considerat sunt diversae scientiae. . ." Sent. Ethic., I,1,25-27.

Before proceeding to the main conclusions to be drawn from the texts above, we should note two points. The first is that Thomas deals with the nature and method only after he has defined the order which specifies science. The reason for this procedure will be discussed in chapter three. At this point it is sufficient to note that any fundamental discussion abou· science which purports to be according to the mind of Thomas should follow the same procedure.

The second point to note is that, since the orders of reality specify the exercises of reason, one may substitute the term "object" for the term "order". For objects specify cognitive powers or habits. Furthermore, the term "object" may in some cases be substituted for the term "subject". Joseph Owens notes[20] that, while Thomas uses the term "object" to refer to a more generic habitus like the speculative and the practical, he uses the term "subject" to refer to the object of a specific science. Nevertheless, common usage today allows the substitution of object for subject in the case of specific sciences.

Now to the conclusions to be drawn from the texts. When human reason faces reality, which may be things either made by man or not made by man (operables or non-operables), it may either contemplate or establish them. The disjunction is complete. For what other fundamental role can reason play in regard to things? Hence there is no ground which is not covered by either term of the disjunction. Under which term, then, should one place the reality of human operations considered, not to be established, but simply to be contemplated? On the one hand, it would not seem that they can be placed under the practical because nothing is being established in reality. On the other hand, the text mentions only natural things, the non-operable, as an example in the category of the speculative. May human operations speculatively considered also be placed in

---

[20] "St. Thomas Aquinas . . . seems careful in using _subjectum_ in regard to science, even while employing _objectum_ in reference to the more generic 'habitus'. ". . . sic enim se habet subjectum ad scientiam, sicut objectum ad potentiam vel habitudinem." Summa Th., I, 1,7c;7a24." The Doctrine of Being in the Aristotelian Metaphysics, 2nd ed. (Toronto, 1963), p. 36, note 10.

this category? Why not? For the disjunction between
the speculative and the practical concerns the two ways
that reason considers things. Since human operations
are considered speculatively, they should be placed
under speculative science.

Could one, however, maintain that human operations
speculatively considered hold a kind of middle ground?
Could this middle ground constitute a category of
science which is both speculative and practical or speculatively practical? To decide this matter let us consider another text, which deals explicitly with the
twofold distinction between the speculative and the
practical sciences.

> The theoretical or speculative intellect is
> properly distinguished from the operative or
> practical intellect by the fact that the
> speculative intellect has for its goal the
> truth which it considers, but the practical
> intellect directs the truth it considers
> towards operation as to its goal. So the
> philosopher says in the De Anima that they
> differ from each other by their goals; and
> in the Metaphysics he states that "the
> goal of practical knowledge is action."[21]

Here St. Thomas, citing Aristotle, employs a different terminology from that used in his commentary on
the Ethics. The meaning, however, is the same. If
speculative reason has for its goal the truth which it
considers, this goal is complete and so does not look
to any other goal outside of itself. Accordingly,
speculative reason does not make but only contemplates
its object. On the other hand, if the goal of practical reason is to direct the truths it considers for

---

[21]"Dicendum quod theoricus sive speculativus intellectus in hoc proprie ab operativo sive practico
distinguitur quod speculativus habet pro fine veritatem quam considerat, practicus vero veritatem consid-
eratam ordinat in operationem tamquam in finem. Et
ideo dicit Philosophus in III De Anima quod differunt
ad invicem fine, et in II Metaphysicae dicitur quod,
'finis speculativae est veritas, sed finis operativae
scientiae est actio'." St. Thomas Aquinas, Expositio
Super Librum Boethii de Trinitate, ed. Bruno Decker
(Leiden, 1955), Q.5, art.1c, p. 164. My translation.

the sake of action, it seeks to establish the realities it considers.[22]

Thomas next proceeds to discuss the types of material which reason must consider to attain its goal.

> Since the material should be proportionate to the goal, the material of the practical sciences should be those things which come into existence through our own activity; thus the knowledge of them can be directed to operation as to its goal. But the material of the speculative sciences should be things which are not coming into existence through our activity. Hence the consideration of them cannot be directed towards operation as to its goal.[23]

The material used in any kind of activity should have a proportion to the goal of that activity. For example, if the activity is the making of a saw, the material used should be a hard substance like iron, which has the capacity of being used to attain the particular goal in question. On the basis of this general principle Thomas argues that the material considered in practical sciences should be those things which come into existence through man's activity. Why? The goal of these sciences is operation or action. Now the only things having the capacity to be enacted are human operations or their products. Consequently only these things can serve as the material for the practical sciences.

---

[22]The basic reason why the object and the goal of the activity of science is identical is because the activity of knowing is identical with what is known which, in turn, is identical with the goal of knowing. See below, page 64, note 35.

[23]"Cum ergo oporteat materiam fini esse proportionatam, oportet practicarum scientiarum materiam esse res illas quae a nostro opere fieri possunt, ut sic earum cognitio in operationem quasi in finem ordinari possit. Speculativarum vero scientiarum materiam oportet esse res quae a nostro opere non fiunt; unde earum consideratio in operationem ordinari non potest sicut in finem." St. Thomas Aquinas, Expositio . . . De Trin., Q.5, art. 1c, p. 164. My translation.

What, then, is the object of practical science? The object which formally specifies the activity by which practical reason attains its goal is not simply human operations but human operations <u>practically</u> <u>considered</u>. By themselves human operations are just the material (or the material object) having the capacity to be considered either speculatively or practically. But when these capacities are actualized by speculative and practical considerations, one then has two distinct formal objects.[24] These formal objects may be called simply objects. For the object of science is a form specifying a cognitive habit.

Thomas moves on to say that the material considered in the speculative sciences should be "things which are not coming into existence through man's activity." Why? The goal of speculative science is not to cause but simply to contemplate its material. Thus its material does not come into existence through this contemplative activity. What kinds of material, then, are suitable for speculative consideration? Natural and divine things are certainly suitable. And because they do not have even the capacity to be caused by man, they are the material only for speculative consideration.

---

[24]Other authors, Henri Renard for example, differ with the above position. He says: "Obviously, the subject matter, which philosophers call the material object, will be for the <u>Philosophy</u> <u>of</u> <u>Morality</u>, the free acts of man, the human acts." After stating that these human acts will not be examined for their ontological reality, but rather from the different formality of their morality, he concludes: "The formal object of our study is, therefore, the human act as moral." <u>The</u> <u>Philosophy</u> <u>of</u> <u>Morality</u>, (Milwaukee, 1953), p.3. For St. Thomas, however, the formal object of ethics is the human act considered for the sake of action. The formality here is simply practical while that of Renard is speculative. For the study of human acts from the viewpoint either of their "ontological reality" or of their morality is a speculative inquiry if the goal is simply the truth. If the inquiry is practical, then the formal object is human acts considered, not as something moral, but as something to be done. The formality of action includes morality. But the formality of morality does not necessarily include action. Cannot one consider the morality of human acts simply for the sake of truth?

Yet human operations may also serve as the material for speculative science because, being entities, they may also be contemplated.[25] In fact, one only discovers the powers and nature of man by analyzing his operations. Obviously these operations are not caused by the analysis. Thus they fit under the description of "things which are not coming into existence through man's activity."

The conclusion of this section is that, because St. Thomas defines moral philosophy in the light of a radical distinction between speculative and practical science, the object of moral science is, not human operations speculatively considered, but human operations practically considered. Hence moral science is simply practical in nature and synthetic in method.

II.   The Threefold Division of Knowledge

The purpose of this section is to lay before the reader a text in which Thomas speaks of a threefold division of knowledge. The reader should then be able to follow better the views of the commentators to be treated in section III. Since this same text will be examined in more detail in chapter two, only a brief outline of it will be given here.

As was mentioned before,[26] Thomas began the question in the Summa Theol. I,14,16 saying that, while some knowledge is speculative only and other knowledge is practical only, there is a knowledge which is speculative in a way (secundum aliquid) and practical in a way (secundum aliquid). On the one extreme, which is speculative only, is the knowledge of things which are not operable (producible) by the knower, such as divine

---

[25]"The practical intellect pertains to those things whose principles are within us not in any manner whatsoever, but as being capable of being executed by us. Hence . . . we can also have speculative knowledge of those things whose causes are within us." St. Thomas Aquinas, The Disputed Questions of Truth, transl. by Robert Mulligan, vol. I, (Chicago, 1952), art.3, q.3, ad 4, p. 154.

[26]p. 3.

things in the case of a human knower and God's own
nature in the case of a divine knower. On the other
extreme, which is practical only, is the knowledge of
human operations which is used to realize some goal.
In the middle category is the knowledge of human operations which is considered for the sake of truth; i.e.,
the knowledge of the operable speculatively considered.

This middle category contains two types of knowledge. An example of the first is:

> if a builder consider a house by defining and
> dividing, and considering what belongs to it
> in general: for this is to consider operable
> things in a speculative manner, and not as
> practically operable; for operable means the
> application of form to matter, and not the
> resolution of a composite into its universal
> formal principles.[27]

In contrasting a house considered speculatively
with a house considered practically, the text gives one
an excellent idea of the contrast between the operable
considered speculatively and practically. A house considered speculatively is viewed as a composite which is
analyzed into its basic formal principles, which are
its causes. In other words, the house is defined. This
way of looking at a house is characteristic of the way
speculative science looks at its own object. It starts
its reasoning from the fact that there is a composite
effect in question. In seeking to reach the truth
about its causes, it analyzes the composite and reduces
it to its simple elements or causes. "In speculative
science," as St. Thomas notes, "it is necessary to proceed in an analytic manner by resolving the composite
into its simple causes . . . " (I,3,57-58).

In the second case, a house is looked upon as a
form which is to be applied to matter. Here the house
is not considered as a composite effect but rather as
an exemplary cause. This form existing in the mind of
the builder is to be taken by him and applied to the
details of production in order to produce an actual

---

[27]Translation by English Dominicans, Benziger,
1947.

house. This way of looking at the house is characterist
of the way practical science looks at the operable.
It starts its reasoning from the fact that some general
form of an operable exists in the mind of an agent who
wishes to make it a reality. Since this form is initial
ly general in nature, the thinker seeks to make it more
specific by applying it to the details of action. When
he has attained a specific notion of exactly what he
wishes to do, he proceeds to act. Intellectually, then,
the agent who possesses science goes through a synthetic
process of reasoning. He starts with a simple notion
of what is to be done, the exemplary cause, and progressively makes it more specific until it is a suitable
guide to action. According to St. Thomas this synthetic
method is "the application of universal and simple
principles to the particular and the composite which
is action" (I,3,52-56).

An example of the second type of knowledge in the
middle category is:

> if a builder should consider how a house can
> be made, not ordering this to the end of
> operation, but only to know how to do it,
> this would be only a speculative consider-
> ation as regards the end, although it con-
> cerns an operable thing.[28]

Here a builder considers a house, not for the sake
of defining it, but to understand how it can be made.
But since he does not actually intend to build the
house, his knowledge is speculative according to end,
which is simply knowledge for its own sake.

The text above may be outlined as follows. In the
first division is the knowledge of the non-operable.
This is purely speculative. In the middle division,
the partly speculative and the partly practical, there
are two kinds of knowledge: the speculative according
to manner and the speculative according to end. In the
last division is the knowledge of the operable practically considered, which is purely practical knowledge.

What has been referred to as a threefold division

---

[28]Translation by the English Dominicans, Benziger,
1947.

of knowledge, then, is really a fourfold division. For the middle category, the operable speculatively considered, has two parts.

According to the argument in section I, a science is either speculative or practical. Therefore one should place both forms of the middle category, the operable speculatively considered, under the generic object of speculative science. The operable practically considered, the fourth division, will be the object of practical science. Consequently, moral science will be simply practical in nature and synthetic in method.

What will happen, however, if one makes the third division of knowledge, one form of the operable speculatively considered, the object of practical science? He will include the first two divisions under speculative science and the fourth division under a type of knowledge which is not scientific. This knowledge will be experience in the case of production and prudence in the case of morals. Thus there will still be only a twofold division of the sciences into speculative and practical. But practical science will now be partly speculative and partly practical in nature. Its method will be mixed. Moral science, then, will be of the same nature.

At issue here are two very different notions of practical and, hence, of moral science. Which notion do the commentators have?

III. The Views of the Three Commentators

To prepare the way for his definition of moral science Lottin gives the following analysis of the text from the Summa I,14,16.

> Knowledge is evidently purely theoretical when it relates to an object which is not itself matter for action, as the knowledge of the things of nature. But it still remains theoretical when its object is without doubt a matter for action but is considered only in a speculative manner, such as the knowledge of a building whose structure is studied.[29]

---

[29]"La connaissance est évidement purement théorique quand elle se rapporte à un objet qui n'est pas de soi matière d'action, telle la connaissance des êtres de la

Lottin includes the first and second divisions of knowledge listed in the Summa under the object of speculative science. In the fourth division, the purely practical, Lottin places the knowledge "which is directed only to action, tending to realize here and now an object which is matter for action."[30] This is the object, not of a science, but of experience in productive matters and of prudence in moral matters.

There remains only the third division of knowledge. About this knowledge Lottin says:

> Between the two extremes there lies the knowledge which, on the one hand, is not in fact directed towards action but, on the other hand, is able to be. And this capability of being directed towards action is more or less proximate.[31]

He gives medicine as an example, citing a text from St. Thomas. St. Thomas, referring to the fact that medicine is divided into a theoretical and a practical part, states that this division "is made on the basis of whether what is studied in medicine is proximate to or remote from practice."[32]

Having interpreted the text from the Summa, Lottin poses the following question about the nature of moral science:

---

nature; mais elle reste théorique encore quand son objet est sans doute matiere d'action mais n'est envisagé que d'une manière spéculative, telle la connaissance d'un édifice dont on étudie la structure." Principes de morale, p. 15.

[30]" . . . laquelle n'est orientée que vers l'action, tendant à réaliser hic et nunc un objet qui est matiere d'action." Principes de morale, p. 15.

[31]"Entre ces deux extrèmes se gliss la connaissance qui, d'une part, n'est pas, de fait, orientée vers l'action mais qui, d'autre part, peut l'être; et cette 'orientabilité' vers l'action est plus ou moins prochaine." Ibid., p. 16.

[32]"St. Thomas Aquinas, Expos. . . . . De Trin., Q.V, art.1, ad 4, p. 170. English translation from The Division and Methods of the Sciences, trans. Armand Maurer, 3rd ed., (Toronto, 1963), p. 14.

. . . without doubt, moral science is not
purely practical for it does not direct knowledge for actions to be done in the here
and now, as prudence does; but is it purely
theoretical or rather does it rest, like
medicine, between the two extremes?[33]

Excluding moral science from the fourth division,
the purely practical, Lottin asks whether moral science
is to be found either in the speculative, the first two
divisions, or in the third division, the partly speculative and the partly practical? The answer to the
question is found in the following:

Moral science is at once both theoretical and
practical. Thus it is first necessary to inquire into the theory of morality, that is to
say the conditions required for a human act
to be morally good; then one must inquire
into the practice of morality in order to
know the way one acquires and organizes a
life that is morally good. Consequently,
there are two parts: the theory of the moral
life and the practice of moral life.[34]

Lottin, then, locates moral science in the category
of the partly speculative and the partly practical.
One part looks to the theoretical foundations while the
other part looks to practice.

_____

[33]" . . . sans doute, la science morale n'est pas
purement pratique car elle n'oriente pas la connaissance
à l'action à poser _hic et nunc_, comme le fait la prudence; mais est-elle purement théorique, ou bien
chemine-t-elle, comme la médicine, entre les deux ex-
trêmes?" _Principes de morale_, p. 16.

[34]"La science morale . . . est à la fois théorique
et pratique. Il faut donc d'abord s'enquérir de la
theorie de la moralité, c'est-à-dire des conditions
requises pour qu'un acte humain soit moralement bon;
il importe ensuite d'envisager la pratique de la moralité, à savoir la manière dont s'aquiert et s'organise
une vie moralement bonne. De là deux parties: la
théorie de la vie morale: la pratique de la vie morale."
Ibid., p. 43.

What is the method of this science? Lottin asks:
"Does one in moral science adopt the synthetic method,
which proceeds by deduction from causes to effects; or
the analytic method, which mounts by induction from
effects to causes?"[35] (The reader should note that the
synthetic method which Lottin is thinking of here is
the one employed in theology and mathematics. Though
this method, as we shall see later,[36] shares the same
name as the method which St. Thomas maintains is used
in practical science, each is quite different in nature.)
Lottin answers that by using a method "which is a real
psychological or metaphysical induction, one can hope
to establish the ontological principles, the objective
foundations of the moral order."[37] The method then of
the theoretical part of morals is analytic. By this
method one discovers not only "the philosophical foundations of the moral order: what is the true foundation
of the moral order; what are the true sanctions of the
moral order . . . ?"[38] One also discovers "the propositions which relate to the rules of action: what
actions, for example, are truly permitted, forbidden,
advised, counseled or warned against by the moral
law. . . ."[39]

For the practical part of the science Lottin, although he does not explicitly address himself to the

---

[35]"Convient-il, en philosophie morale, d'adopter la
méthod synthetique procédant par déduction, des cause
aux effets; ou la méthode analytique remontant, par induction, des effets aux causes?" Ibid., p. 43.

[36]See below, chapter 5, p.

[37]". . . qui est un véritable induction psycholo-
gique ou métaphysique, on peut espérer établir les
principes ontologiques, les fondement objectifs de
l'ordre moral." Ibid., p. 49.

[38]". . . les fondements philosophiques de l'ordre
moral: quelle est la vraie norme de moralité, quel est
la véritable fondement de l'obligation morale; quelles
sont les vraies sanctions de l'ordre moral?" Ibid., p.22.

[39]". . . les unes se rapportent aux règles de l'agir
humain: quelles actions, par example, sont vraiment
prescrites, défendues, permises, conseillées, décon-
seillées par la loi morale. . . ." Ibid., p. 22.

question, would seem to use the practical method. He says that "after speculative reason has proven that theft is truly a moral evil, practical reason dictates the prohibition of theft."[40] This imperative or "norm is the object of reason, certainly not of purely speculative reason, but of reason turned to action, not however towards a concrete action to be done hic et nunc. This acquiescence of reason still sees an action impersonally, but it is already practical."[41] The method, then, of the practical part of morals is to apply general truths to the realm of action. This realm, however, is not seen as that of the particular as such, which is ruled by prudence, but as the realm of specific rules which pertain to all men in an impersonal way. For Lottin, the method of moral science is both analytic and synthetic.

Since the manner in which one defines the nature of any science will determine the relationship of that science to the others, the final question to be put to Lottin is about the relationship of moral philosophy to speculative science. He says:

> Looking at these two classes of propositions, why can I not set up a treatment of morals whose end is to make clear to my students the principles or, if one wishes, the theory of the moral order. Thus even when I, in attaching myself to the most abstract part of morals, force myself to examine the ultimate foundations of the moral order, am I not doing a work of moral science or, if one wishes, of metamorals, and so of moral science?[42]

---

[40] " . . . après que la raison théorique a prouvé que vol est vraiment un mal moral, la raison pratique dicte la prohibition du vol ...." Ibid., p. 23.

[41] "Cette norme est objet de raison, non certes de raison surement spéculative, mais de raison tournée vers l'action, non toutefois vers une action concrete à poser hic et nunc. Cet acquiescement de la raison vise un agir impersonel encore, mais il est déjà pratique." Ibid., p. 23.

[42] "Envisageant ces deux classes de propositions sous l'angle exclusif de leur vérité, pourquoi ne

Lottin maintains that one may examine the propositions in the theoretical part of morals simply for the sake of truth. In this examination the teacher would be dealing with the basic principles or ultimate foundations of the moral order. One may conclude, then, that such an inquiry would require that the nature of man, a non-operable treated in purely speculative science, would have to be known by the moral philosopher. Moral philosophy, then, would be ultimately and directly dependent upon purely speculative science for foundations. Thus if one wished to have a fully scientific grasp of moral science, he would have to be master of metaphysics. For how could one be said to be a master of moral science if he did not fully grasp the first principles of that science?

If the first principles of moral science are found in metaphysics, one may conclude then that the moral philosopher need not necessarily be a prudent man at least as far as the foundations are concerned. For the possession of speculative science does not essentially entail the possession of prudence.

This examination of the views of Lottin shows that he has interpreted the text from the _Summa_ in a way which follows the second of the two schemas presented earlier.[43] Consequently he reaches conclusions about moral science which appear to differ with those of St. Thomas.

***

The next commentator to be examined is John of St. Thomas, whose views are found in his work the _Cursus_

---

pourrais-je pas constituer un enseignement de la morale dans la but de faire comprendre a mes élèves les prin-́ cipes ou, si l'on veut, la théorie de l'ordre moral? Alors même que, m'attachant à la partie la plus abstraite de la morale, je m'efforce de scruter les fondements derniers de l'ordre moral, ne fais-je pas oeuvre de science morale, de métamorale, si l'on veut, et donc de philosophie morale?" _Ibid._, p. 22-23.

[43]See above, p. 14.

Philosophicus Thomisticus.[44] One indication of the
great influence of this commentator is that the Ars
Logica of this work has been published in an English
translation entitled The Material Logic of John of St.
Thomas.[45] Maritain has written the preface and Yves
Simon is one of the translators. Another indication of
great influence is that, according to Lottin,[46] Joseph
Gredt and L. Thiry accept John's views on moral
philosophy.

How does John of St. Thomas interpret the text
from the Summa? After referring the reader to basic
texts from Aristotle and St. Thomas, he concludes that
"the speculative looks to the truth in order to know
and the practical looks to the truth in order that it
may come about and be put into execution in a work."[47]
How does he interpret this twofold division of the
speculative and the practical? A little later he says:

> For knowledge to be speculative, it is required
> either that its material be not operable, as
> in the case of God, the angels, or the heavens
> or, if it is an operable, that it be attained,
> not as an operable, but as knowledge and as
> a kind of truth. On the other hand, for know-
> ledge to be practical, it is required that the

---

[44]Joannis a Santo Thomas, Cursus Philosophicus
Thomisticus, ed. B. Rieser, vol. I, Ars Logica (Turin,
1930).

[45]John of St. Thomas, The Material Logic of John
of St. Thomas, tr. Yves Simon et al. (Chicago, 1955).

[46]"Les vues de Jean de Saint-Thomas ont ete reprises
par le P.J. Gredt O.S.B., Elementa Philosophiae Aristo-
telico-thomisticae, Freib. i. B, t. I, 1929, no. 103--
Et c'est sans doute dans la meme sens que s'oriente dom
L. Thiry . . . ." Odon Lottin, Principes de morale,
p. 17, n.2. The work of L. Thiry is Speculativum- practicum secundum S. Thomam quo modo se habeant in actu
humano (Studia Anselmiana, fac. 9) Rome, 1939.

[47]"Et consistit in hoc, quod speculativum respicit
veritatem, ut sciatur, practicum vero, ut fiat et
executioni mandetur in opere." Cursus Phil., II P.,
Q.1, art.4, p. 269. All translations of John of St.
Thomas are mine.

material be an operable and that it be
attained as an operable.[48]

Here John of St. Thomas divides knowledge in the
threefold way. The first way is speculative knowledge
of the non-operable and is the object of purely speculative science. The second way is speculative knowledge
of the operable and is the object, as we shall soon
see, of moral science. The third way is practical knowledge of the operable which, as we shall also see, is
the object of prudential, not scientific knowledge.
Without saying so, John of St. Thomas is following the
text from the Summa.

In the light of this threefold division John of
St. Thomas speaks of moral science as follows:

> Moral science may be considered in two ways:
> first, as it includes prudence; second, as it
> excludes it and is solely concerned with the
> knowledge of virtue in the speculative manner.
> The first way has the nature of practical know-
> ledge because of prudence, which it includes,
> and uses the practical principle "good is
> to be done" in a practical way.[49]

Considered as including prudence, moral science is
practical because it uses practical principles in a
practical way. But what is the nature of moral science
if it is taken strictly as a science? It is a speculative science because, in excluding prudence, "it is
solely concerned with the knowledge of virtue in a
speculative manner."

---

[48]"unde ut sit speculativum, requiritur, quod vel
materia eius operabilis non sit, sicut qui considerat
Deum et angelum aut coelum etc., vel si sit operabile,
non ut operabile, sed ut scibile et tamquam verum quod-
dam attingatur. Ut autum sit practicum, requiritur, ut
materia sit operabilis et ut modo operabili attingatur."
Cursus Phil., II P., Q.1, art.4, p. 276.

[49]"Scientia moralis potest dupliciter considerari:
uno modo, ut etiam includit prudentiam, alio modo, ut
eam excludit et solum versatur circa cognitionem virtutum speculando. Primo modo habet rationem practici ex
parte prudentiae, quam includit, et utitur illo principio practico: 'Bonum est faciendum' modo practico."
Ibid., II P., Q.1, art.4, p. 276.

The text continues, establishing without doubt the above conclusion.

> If moral science excludes prudence and only treats of the matter of virtue by defining, dividing, etc., it is speculative knowledge. . . . For it does not use practical principles in a practical way, i.e., as causing motion and affective inclination, but in a speculative way, insofar as they know the nature of virtue and of prudence from the point of view of their truth, as can be seen in the Ethics. . . . And so one may well be a noted philosopher and theologian while being an imprudent sinner.[50]

John of St. Thomas holds, then, that moral science is speculative in nature and analytic in method. As an example of this type of moral science, he gives the Ethics of Aristotle. Since the Ethics is supposedly an example of speculative science, one may be an expert in this science while being an imprudent sinner. In brief, the moral philosopher need not be a prudent man.

The text continues:

> There is nothing absurd about the conclusion that there is no practical science, if science is taken in its strict and proper sense, because science proceeds by analysis and definition while practical knowledge proceeds by moving and synthesis.[51]

---

[50]"Si vero scientia moralis secludat prudentiam et solum tractet de materia virtutum definiendo, dividendo etc., est speculativa . . . . Nec utitur principiis practicis aut modo practico, id est ut moventibus et inclinantibus affective, sed praecise speculativis, quatenus cognoscunt naturam virtutum et prudentiae in ratione veri, ut in Ethicis . . . videri potest. Et ita bene potest aliquis esse insignis philosophus ethicus et theologus et imprudens peccator. Ibid., II P., Q.1, art.4, p. 277.

[51]"Neque est inconveniens, quod non detur scientia practica, si vere et proprie scientia est, quia scientia procedit resolvendo et definiendo, practica movendo et componendo." Cursus Phil., II P., Q.1, art.4, p. 277.

In denying that there is such a thing as a practical science, John of St. Thomas seems to be disregarding both Aristotle and St. Thomas, a fact noted by his editors.[52]

At any rate, John of St. Thomas reasons that if a science is truly scientific, it proceeds by analysis and, therefore, cannot be practical. On the other hand,

---

[52]Concerning this point, his editors say: "This view is thoroughly unaristotelian and constitutes a paradox never fully explained." The editors then present their own views. These will be quoted in full because they are typical of many Thomists. "True, the theory of the practical sciences in Aristotle is far from clear. Referring to the basic treatment of the intellectual habitus in Ethics 6, let it be said that the Aristotelian notion of science applies primarily to sciences that are unqualifiedly and exclusively theoretical, whereas the Aristotelian notion of practical knowledge applies primarily to a knowledge that is unqualifiedly practical, in other words, to prudential knowledge. A practical science is necessarily an ambiguous entity, less scientific than a theoretical science, less practical than a prudential habitus, and bearing the mark of a sort of compromise. It is a mixed case, which can be expected to involve more obscurity than simple cases." The Material Logic of John of St. Thomas, pp. 592-593. Along a similar vein John Naus says: " . . . analogy has appeared again and again in the course of our study. It was especially in evidence in chapter four where gradations of cognition became progressively more practical as they departed from the prime analogate of strictly speculative knowledge to approach the prime analogate of strictly practical knowledge. Paradoxes follow quite naturally from such analogy: practical science is in a way speculative; theoretical science can be practical as to its object.." The Nature of the Practical Intellect According to St. Thomas Aquinas, p. 201. Similarly, William A. Wallace notes: "Practical science is not completely practical knowledge, and in this it is distinguished from prudence, and at the same time it is not completely speculative knowledge . . . ." The Role of Demonstration in Moral Theology, p. 79.

if knowledge is truly practical, it proceeds by synthesis and, therefore, cannot be scientific. Consequently, when moral science is considered as including prudence, "it is identical with prudence and so does not belong to the speculative habits but to the practical ones . . . ."[53] If it is considered as excluding prudence, it is not practical.

What is the relationship between moral philosophy and purely speculative science? John of St. Thomas answers:

> If moral science is understood speculatively, that is, as dealing with the nature of virtue, then it pertains to Philosophy and is part of it because, since it deals with the rational soul, it follows that one must also treat of its moral acts.[54]

The reasoning here is quite consistent. If moral science is understood speculatively, human operations are considered for the sake of truth. Consequently, operations are analyzed until a clear idea of their cause is attained, i.e., the human soul. But the soul is a non-operable and, therefore, treated in purely speculative science (philosophy). Consequently, moral science is part of speculative science. In other words, purely speculative science contains the foundations or first principles[55] of moral science.

---

[53]"Scientia autem moralis si sumatur practice, est idem quod prudentia, et sic non pertinet ad habitus speculativos, sed practicos . . ." Cursus Phil., II P., Q.27, art.1, p. 826.

[54]"Si vero sumatur speculative pro scientia ethica, quae tractat de natura virtutum, sic pertinet ad Philosophiam et est pars illius, quia cum agat de anima intellectiva, consequenter de moralibus eius debet tractare." Cursus Phil., II P., Q.27, art.1, pp. 826-827. Cf. J. Gredt: ". . . Ethicam subaltenari tertiae Philosophiae naturalis parti, quae est de anima." Elementa Philosophiae, (Frib., 1937), 7th ed., vol. II, p. 303, no. 879.

[55]Further clarification of the term "principle" will be made in the due course of the argument. For now it is sufficient to note that a principle is any kind of

Like Lottin, John of St. Thomas places moral science in the middle category of the threefold division of knowledge, which is called speculative in a way and practical in a way. Unlike Lottin, however, he maintains that this category is speculative. He maintains that "no science can be both speculative and practical."[56] Consequently, John of St. Thomas holds that moral science is speculative in nature, analytic in method and part of purely speculative science. Furthermore, the moral philosopher need not be a prudent man.

Clearly, there is nothing haphazard about the reasoning of John of St. Thomas. Once he has determined that the object of moral science is operations speculatively considered, he rigorously draws all the consequences. In this review the rigor of the argument has only been indicated. It will remain for later chapters to show, once the object has been determined, the consequences flow necessarily. At the very least, however, one may conclude that John of St. Thomas appears to differ quite significantly from his master.

***

The last commentator to be reviewed is Jacques Maritain. His teaching on the nature of moral science is quite detailed and precise as far as his stance towards the teaching of St. Thomas is concerned. And the basic thrust of Maritain's teaching is the same from the first edition of The Degrees of Knowledge in 1932 to the authoritative English translation in 1959.[57] We will concern ourselves with this last edition.

---

source, beginning or starting point. Aristotle defines it as follows: "It is common, then, to all beginnings to be the first point from which a thing either is or comes to be or is known . . . ." Metaphys. 5,1,1073a 17-19. In reference to a science, a principle can be either the fact from which originates one's knowledge of the cause or the cause from which originates the effect.

[56]"Non posse unicam scientiam naturalis ordinis simul esse practicam et speculativam. . . ." Cursus Phil., II P., Q.1, art.4, p. 270.

[57]This translation was undertaken with the close

Leaving aside for the moment Maritain's view of the text from the <u>Summa</u>, let us inquire into his attitude towards John of St. Thomas. The latter seems to have eliminated the notion of a practical science. With some hesitation, Maritain nevertheless holds that the eminent commentator has preserved the practical character of moral science. On this issue he is opposed by Simon,[58] who agrees with the basic stance of Maritain on most points, and by Lottin,[59] who differs with Maritain on many points.

At any rate, Maritain makes his own position quite clear:

> However, lest a hasty reading of the above-quoted text of John of St. Thomas lead us astray, and lest we imagine that moral philosophy is a purely and simply speculative science, a metaphysics or a psychology of the virtues, we must remember that, as St. Thomas repeatedly teaches, the reason why practical philosophy is distinguished essentially from speculative philosophy, is that it is from the very outset directed towards operation . . . and considers the operable <u>insofar as it is operable</u>. His italics. (p. 457)

---

collaboration of Maritain himself, as his Foreward indicates. All references are taken from this edition and will be placed in the body of the text.

[58]"Entièrement d'accord avec M. Maritain sur le fond de la question, nous n'interprétons pas tout à fait de la même manière que lui les texts de la <u>Logique</u> de Jean de s. Thomas. M. Maritain paraît en effet admettre--avec un peu d'hésitation d'ailleurs--que dans la pensée de Jean de s. Thomas la philosophie morale conserverait le charactère essentiellement pratique qu'elle possède à coup sûr chez Aristote et s. Thomas. Nous croyon au contraire que Jean de s. Thomas, sans équivoque possible, attribue à la philosophie morale un charactere scientifique tout speculatif. . . ." Y. Simon, <u>Critique de la connaissance morale</u>, p. 90n.

[59]"Cet exposé passerait difficilement pour un écho fidèle des déclarations du Commentaire sur l'<u>Ethique</u> de Saint Thomas." <u>Principes de morale</u>, p. 17.

While John of St. Thomas appears to have restricted the treatment of the operable as operable to the virtue of prudence, thus relegating moral science to the category of the speculative, Maritain very definitely considers that moral science also treats of this object. Thus moral science is definitely practica.

Maritain holds that the operable considered as operable is a kind of generic object including three more specific objects:

> . . . the operable thing can be considered, precisely as operable, in three different ways: from the point of view of knowledge, considered above all as knowing, or consider- ed as already operating also, or considered above all as operating. (p.458)

The knowledge of the human act "considered above all as knowing" will prove to be the object of specu- latively practical moral science. The knowledge of human acts "considered as already operating" will prove to be the object of practically practical moral science And the knowledge of human acts "considered above all as operating" will be the object of prudence. For Maritain, then, there are degrees within the general category of the practical.

The points above are supported by the following text. Referring to the knowledge possessed by such guides as John of the Cross and St. Alphonsus, Maritain says:

> . . . in the philosophical order, in which habitus are more distinct, we regard it as probable that such a practical science con- stitutes a habitus specifically distinct from that of moral philosophy. For although the fundamentally speculative structure of the means of knowledge used by moral philos- ophy does not suffice to classify this latter in the speculative order, for the reason that these means are themselves in- volved in the typical movement of a knowledge which is characterized first and foremost by its practical finality, the fact remains that within the genus, practical, a dif- ferent notional structure and a different mode of defining should denote a specific

diversity . . . . Therefore we do not
think that it is enough to say that the
strictly practical moral sciences are simply
particular developments of the habitus of
moral philosophy. They must differ specifically from this habitus. (p.464)

Maritain maintains that in the philosophical, as
opposed to the theological order, there are two distinct moral sciences. There is the speculatively
practical which, though speculative in its intellectual
structure, is practical in its finality. And there is
practically practical moral science, which is not
simply a development of moral philosophy, but
specifically distinct.

In his work <u>Science</u> <u>and</u> <u>Wisdom</u> one can find the
same insistence on two distinct practical sciences:

In the philosophical order . . . specula-
tively-practical knowledge and practically-
practical knowledge are specifically distinct,
just as, in speculative philosophy, at the
first degree of abstraction, the philosophy
of nature and the sciences of phenomena
constitute two sciences specifically
distinct.[60]

It is not our concern to explore the full ramifi-
cations of what Maritain means by two specifically
distinct moral sciences. Indeed, as Ralph McInerny
notes: "It is no easy matter to grasp precisely what
it is that Maritain means by the 'practically practical'
as opposed to the 'speculatively practical' and to
'prudence."[61] It is our concern, however, to note
how Maritain sees his teaching in relationship to that
of St. Thomas. Maritain is quite clear on this matter.

The distinction between speculatively-
practical moral knowing and the practically-
practical moral science seems to be solidly

---

[60]J. Maritain, <u>Science</u> <u>and</u> <u>Wisdom</u>, tr. by Bernard
Wall (New York, 1940), p. 138 n.2.

[61]Ralph McInerny, "The Degrees of Practical Know-
ledge", <u>Conference-Seminar</u> on <u>Jacques</u> <u>Maritain's</u> <u>The</u>
<u>Degrees</u> <u>of</u> <u>Knowledge</u>, (St. Louis, 1981), p. 123-124.

based on St. Thomas' principles, though as far as I know, St. Thomas never explicitly formulated it. His own plan of thought was that of speculative science and speculatively practical science.[62]

For Maritain, then, moral science as defined in the commentary on the Ethics is speculatively practical in nature.

What texts does Maritain use to justify his position?

With regard to the exegesis of the texts of St. Thomas on practical knowledge, my remarks on question 14, article 16, of the Summa are also valid for the corresponding passage in De Veritate, q.3, art.3. The science in which the res operabilis non consideratur ut est operabilis does not correspond to moral philosophy (speculatively practical) but is a pure speculative science (ibid., ad 2). In the thought of St. Thomas, it is a matter of God's speculative knowledge of created things. And hence the scientia habitualiter practica which Thomas speaks of in ad 2 does not correspond to what we call practically-practical moral science, but to moral science in general (both speculative and practical).[63]

In brief, Maritain considers (quite correctly) that the third division of knowledge in the Summa I,14,16, the operable considered speculatively according to end, is equivalent to the scientia habitualiter practica in the De Veritate 3,3. But these descriptions are taken to apply to practical and, hence, to moral science. On this point Maritain agrees with Lottin.

Having made a distinction between the objects and natures of moral science, Maritain quite consistently carried out this distinction into the methods of these studies. After noting that the method proper to all

_____

[62]Science and Wisdom, p.138 n.2.

[63]Ibid., p.138 n.2.

types of practical knowledge is "the practical and composite mode" (p.457), Maritain explains the method proper to speculatively practical science.

> . . . what moral philosophy thus prepares and gathers up in view of operations to be directed from afar, is knowledge whose structure is wholly intellectual, whose truth implies neither regulation by right appetite nor affective motion, and which examines its different objects according to the laws of ontological analysis, <u>dividendo et resolvendo</u>, in order to grasp their intelligible constituent. Thus in moral philosophy the mode of science is not practical but speculative <u>as to the fundamental equipment of knowledge and as to the structure of notions and definitions</u>. His italics.
> (p.457-458)

Within the genus of the composite mode the particular method of speculatively practical science is analytic. The structure of this knowledge is "wholly intellectual, whose truth implies neither regulation by right appetite nor affective motion." In other words, the possessor of this science need not have the virtue of prudence, which regulates man's appetites and will so that he acts in accordance with his knowledge. By this science he simply understands certain truths which guide human action "from afar". Accordingly, as Maritain notes in another place, "the most expert and competent philosopher in ethical matters can be disconcerted by the smallest act to be done, and he himself can lead an immoral life" (p.313). This remark echoes that of John of St. Thomas regarding the science as found in the <u>Ethics</u> of Aristotle.[64]

What is the method of practically practical moral science?

> The whole mode of science here is practical. What does that mean? It means that there is no question here of explaining and resolving a truth, even a practical truth, into its

---

[64] See above, p.22, n.50.

reasons and principles. The question is to prepare for action and to assign its proximate rules. And, since action is a concrete thing which must be thought of in its concretion before being posited in being, knowledge here, instead of analyzing, composes . . . . It is in this wholly characteristic sense that Thomists teach that practical science (practically practical) proceeds modo compositivo like art and prudence. (p.315)

Must the possessor of this science have the virtue of prudence? Maritain states in another place that "strictly practical moral science supposes prudence--(and therefore the other moral virtues)" (p.463).

Though Maritain holds that the moral philosophy explicitly treated by St. Thomas is practical in its finality, it is speculative in its intellectual structure and method and does not require that its possessor be a prudent man. Therefore Maritain sees the need of a practically practical science which is entirely practical in structure and method and requires that its possessor be prudent. This science Maritain sees as implicit in the principles of St. Thomas.

IV. Conclusion

None of the commentators has taken the position that, because of the radical distinction between speculative and practical science, moral science is simply practical both in nature and in method. Using the text from the Summa as the basis for determining what is meant by the distinction between speculative and practical science in the commentary on the Ethics, the commentators arrive at the following conclusions. Lottin holds that moral science is speculative and practical. John of St. Thomas maintains that it is speculative. And Maritain holds that it is speculatively practical. From these conclusions about the object of moral science, there follows consequences about the method of moral science, the relationship of moral science to speculative science, and the relationship of the moral philosopher to the prudent man.

But does the text from the Summa and from related

texts warrant the conclusions of the commentators? To
answer that question the next chapter will examine
these texts to see whether their teaching is consistent
or not with the radical distinction between speculative
and practical science. To put the matter another way:
do these texts show that practical science is simply
or purely practical? Or do they show that practical
science is of a mixed nature?

CHAPTER II

ST. THOMAS' NOTION OF PRACTICAL SCIENCE

The views of the commentators on the following texts are typical of the views of most other commentators in that none, to my knowledge, interprets the texts in the light of a radical distinction between speculative and practical science. Accordingly, this chapter will present extensive excerpts from the text of Thomas and argue from them with only passing references to contrary views. To attempt a fuller treatment of these views, which are strongly influenced by centuries of commentating especially upon the Summa, is beyond the scope of this work.

I.   The Text from the Summa Theol. I,14,16[1]

The question is: "Whether God has speculative knowledge of things?" As one can see, the question deals with a type of practical knowledge, the productive knowledge that God has of His creatures, against the Aristotelian background of the distinction between speculative and practical science.

Setting the stage for the argument, Objection One maintains:

> that God has not a speculative knowledge of things. For the knowledge of God is the cause of things. . . . But speculative knowledge is not the cause of things known. Therefore the knowledge of God is not speculative.

The objection is based on the valid premise that speculative knowledge is not the cause of things. Accepting this premise, St. Thomas will, however, reject the conclusion that God does not have speculative

---

[1]All the texts of the Summa are taken from the translation of the English Dominicans, Benziger, 1947.

knowledge of his creatures. In the process of demonstrating this point, St. Thomas should reveal the basis upon which he distinguishes the speculative from the practical.

Thomas begins his response as follows:

> Some knowledge is speculative only; some is practical only; and some is partly speculative and partly practical. In proof whereof it must be observed that knowledge can be called speculative in three ways. . . .

As was mentioned before,[2] this threefold division of knowledge is really fourfold because the category of the speculative in a way and practical in a way has two parts.

Having announced that knowledge can be called speculative in three ways, Thomas describes the first way:

> first, on the part of the things known, which are not operable by the knower; such is the knowledge of man about natural or divine things.

Non-operables, not capable of being produced by the knower, can be considered only speculatively, as was mentioned earlier.[3] Consequently, this knowledge is called purely speculative.

The second way that knowledge is speculative is

> as regards the manner of knowing--as, for instance, if a builder consider a house by defining and dividing; and considering what belongs to it in general; for this is to consider operable things in a speculative manner, and not as practically operable; for operable means the application of form to

---

[2] See above, p. 14.
[3] See above, p. 10.

matter, and not the resolution of a
composite into its universal formal
principles.

This knowledge is called speculative in regard to
the manner or mode in which it is known because its
material is the operable. Now the operable may be
considered either as something merely to be defined
or as something to be built. The fact that this knowledge is speculative, then, is due to the way the
operable is considered.

Is this second way of considering the material any
different from the way the material is considered in
purely speculative knowledge? No. Both the non-
operable and the operable are considered simply for the
sake of truth. Thus both are equally included under
the generic object of speculative science. But Thomas
calls the first type purely speculative and the second
speculative in regard to manner to indicate a material
or accidental difference between these two objects
which leaves their essential sameness untouched.

The claim that the specific objects of the first
and second type are equally and fundamentally speculative does not do away with the fact that the first includes higher things to contemplate than the second.
For non-operables in reference to man include divine
things while the non-operable in reference to God is,
as we shall see shortly, the divine nature Itself.
Nevertheless, the formal or essential way in which both
the non-operable and the operable are considered makes
them equally objects of contemplation. That the material of the second way is the operable does not make this
object practical in any essential way. If this object
is to be called practical in a way, that way must be
accidental to it.

The third way of knowledge is speculative

> as regards the end; for the practical
> intellect differs from the speculative, as
> the Philosopher says (De Anima III). For
> the practical intellect is ordered to the
> end of the operation; whereas the end of the
> speculative intellect is the consideration
> of truth. Hence if a builder should consider
> how a house can be made, not ordering this
> to the end of operation, but only to know

(how to do it), this would be only a
speculative consideration as regards the
end, although it concerns an operable thing.

Significantly, Thomas begins by citing the twofold distinction between the ends of the intellect.
In view of this distinction, he determines that this
third type of knowledge is speculative according to
end. Here the builder, instead of using his knowledge
of the operable, simply contemplates it.

Why should Thomas call this third type speculative
according to end when, as we have argued, the other two
types have the same end; namely, the truth for its own
sake? The reason is that Thomas thereby intends to
show how the material of the third type differs from
that of the other two types.

In the first type, the material is not even capable
of being produced by the knower. In the second type,
the material is capable of being produced. But the
manner in which this material is known, i.e., by
definition, makes production impossible. For the
knowledge of, for example, the mere definition of a
house is too general ever to be practical. Moreover,
the fact that a man has this knowledge does not necessarily suppose that he has the ability to build one.
There is a great difference between the ability to
frame a definition of a house and to build one.

In the third division the material is not only
capable of being produced. The knower in question is
also capable of producing it. For to know how to build
a house presupposes the practical knowledge and skill
to build it.

There is a great difference, then, between the
specific objects of the three types of knowledge. Yet
these objects all share the following characteristics.
First, the material considered is some type of reality,
either operable or non-operable. Second, the material
is considered simply for the sake of truth. Third,
the knowledge never results in the production of anything. Therefore, all three objects are included under
the generic object of speculative science.

Thomas continues:

Therefore knowledge which is speculative by
reason of the thing itself known, is merely

speculative. But that which is speculative
either in its mode or as to its end is partly speculative and partly practical: and
when it is ordained to an operative end,
it is simply practical.

Having listed the first three ways that knowledge
is speculative, Thomas mentions finally the fourth
way, the simply practical. Here the operable is considered as operable and so is the only way that ever
actually results in the production of anything.

It would seem, then, that the basis here upon
which Thomas divides all knowledge is exactly the same
as the basis upon which he divided the sciences in his
commentaries on the Ethics and on the De Trinitate.
Anything which reason does not establish but merely
considers is the object of speculative science. And
human operations which reason establishes by means of
its considerations are the objects of practical
science.[4] It is true that the texts from the commentaries do not explicitly mention the operable speculatively considered. But they do establish a complete
disjunction between the goals of the speculative and
the practical. And this disjunction in goals places
both the non-operable and the operable speculatively
considered upon one side of the division and the operable considered as operable on the other side.

This disjunction is complete. When a man is
simply contemplating something for what it is, he is
not establishing it by that act. And when a man is

---

[4]After his examination of the text from the commen
tary on the De Trinitate 5,1, Wallace draws a different
conclusion: "From these preliminary indications of St.
Thomas' thought, we can conclude to at least two bases
of distinction between speculative and practical knowledge, one taken from the subject matter with which it
is concerned, the other taken from the end of the knowledge itself; speculative knowledge has for its object
the non-operable, while practical knowledge is concerned with the operable; the end of speculative knowledge is truth, while that of practical knowledge is
operation. Other bases of distinction are implied
also. . . ." The Role of Demonstration in Moral
Theology, p.74.

establishing anything, he is not simply contemplating it. Of course the full proof for the validity of this view about the radical distinction will come when all of the implications of the distinction are drawn out in the course of the argument. So far the argument may seem rather academic. But that is often the case in arguments dealing with first principles.

Yet one cannot deny that St. Thomas calls the second and third divisions of knowledge in the Summa speculative in a way and practical in a way. Does he use this terminology simply to meet the needs of his particular argument here? Such a use is not out of the question. On this view of the matter Thomas could be holding to the radical distinction while adopting a secundum quid terminology to suit his particular needs of the moment.

Or does Thomas mean to show that the second and third divisions constitute a kind of middle ground which admits of varying degrees of the speculative and the practical? In this case, there would be no radical distinction between the sciences. Instead, the division of the purely speculative, not having any degree of the practical in it, would stand as the prime example or analogate[5] of speculative knowledge. The division of the purely practical, not having any degree of the speculative, would stand as the prime analogate of the practical. The second division would be mainly speculative but partially practical. And the third division would be mainly practical but partially speculative.

Furthermore, if there are varying degrees of the speculative and the practical, one would be able to set up a chart listing the various elements that go into knowledge. Under the headings of object, end, mode and knower, one could catalogue the various types of knowledge according as they incorporate one or more of these elements, thus fixing their degree of being speculative and/or practical.[6]

---

[5]See above, p. 23, last half of note 52.

[6]W.A. Wallace, The Role of Demonstration in Moral Theology, p.79. Maritain has a different chart in his The Degrees of Knowledge, p.459.

Rather than attempting to settle these matters now, let us note how Thomas concludes his argument. Seeing the point of the argument, we should be able to judge how he employs his terms and distinctions.

> In accordance with this therefore, it must be said that God has of Himself a speculative knowledge only; for He Himself is not an operable.
> But of all other things He has both speculative and practical knowledge. He has speculative knowledge as regards the mode; for whatever we know speculatively in things by defining and dividing, God knows this much more perfectly.
> Now of things which He can make, but does not make at any time, He has not a practical knowledge, according as knowledge is called practical from the end. But He has a practical knowledge of what He makes in some point in time.

The point that Thomas sets out to prove is that God has speculative knowledge of His creatures. Thus he places this knowledge in a middle category between the purely speculative on the one hand and the purely practical on the other. He calls the middle category practical in a way because its material, being the operable, is different from the non-operable. But this distinction is material or accidental or incidental from the viewpoint of the generic object of the speculative. And he calls the middle category speculative in a way because, though its material is the same as that of the purely practical, the middle category is essentially or formally distinct from the last category.

As one can see, the _secundum_ _quid_ terminology poses no particular problems as long as the essential likeness and difference of the speculative and the practical are kept in mind. In regard to essential likeness and difference, knowledge must be either speculative or practical. In regard to incidental likeness and difference, knowledge may be speculative in one way but practical in another.

The terminology which Thomas uses in this text, then, is perfectly suited to his purposes. Consequently this text does not warrant the conclusion that the distinction between the speculative and the practical is not radical. Therefore, one should not place practical science in the category of the third division. If one places practical science in the category of the operable speculatively considered according to end, one has a knowledge which never results in the production of anything. For neither God nor man produces in this category.

Those who make the third division the object of practical science reserve the category of the purely practical for non-scientific knowledge, which is experience in productive matters and prudence in morals. Is this move warranted by the text? In the very last section of the whole article St. Thomas states: ". . . we must say that perfect knowledge of operable things is obtainable only if they are known in so far as they are operable. Therefore, since the knowledge of God is in every way perfect, He must know what is operable by Him, formally as such, and not only in so far as they are speculative."

Since the knowledge of the operable considered as operable is the perfect form of practical knowledge, it must include not only the experiential knowledge of production but practical science or art as well. For is not the knowledge of an agent who has both art and experience superior to the knowledge of one who has only experience? It would seem, then, that in moral matters the category of the purely practical cannot be reserved only to prudence. Is not knowledge of the practical more perfect when it includes moral science as well as prudence?

In putting both art and moral science in the category of the purely practical, we are assuming that these have the same ends as practical experience and prudence. Is such a view valid? Thomas states in another place that:

> in practical matters experience seems to differ in no way from art; for when it comes to acting, the differences between experience and art, which is a difference between the singular and the universal, disappears, because art operates with reference to singulars, just as experience does. Therefore the aforesaid difference pertains only to

the way in which they come to know.[7]

Experience and art have the same end, the operable considered as operable. Yet they are distinct ways of knowing. The same teaching would seem to apply to moral science and prudence. This point, however, will be taken up later on in chapter three.[8]

Again, if one places practical science in the third rather than in the fourth division, he is overlooking a basic fact about practical knowledge. Practical knowledge comes to the agent, not primarily by study, but by practice and long experience. From reflection upon this experience comes art or practical science, which in turn is combined with experience in order to make the agent more effective in production. If, however, the agent has not already acquired experience and art in the realm of the purely practical, he will not be able to be the man of art in the third division who simply contemplates the operable. For this division presupposes that the artist has art but he does not choose to use it.

Now Cajetan holds that, while the knowledge of the third division is speculative due to its end, this end is that of the knower, not that of the knowledge itself. Accordingly, the knowledge itself is practical.[9] On the basis of this type of distinction Maritain claims that the science in this division is practical.[10] But this

---

[7]St. Thomas Aquinas, Commentary on the Metaphysics of Aristotle, trans. by J. Rowan (Chicago, 1961), Bk.I, lect. 1, no. 20, p.12.

[8]See below, pp. 59-61.

[9]" . . . practicum et speculativum hic sumitur non solum ut sunt conditiones scientiae secundum se, sed etiam ex parte scientis. Et propterea dicitur quod ars domificativa non intendentis domificare, est speculativa ex fine . . .: glossandum est enim de fine ex parte scientis, et non ipsius scientiae. Quoniam si loquimur de fine ipsius scientiae, ipsa est etiam practica ex fine. . . ." This text of Cajetan may be found in the Leonine Edition of the Summa Theologiae I,14,16.

[10]Concerning the third division of knowledge in the Summa, Maritain says: " . . . St. Thomas speaks of what is speculative ex fine while thinking of the actual

distinction is not true to the text. Both the end of
the knower and the actual end to which he puts his
knowledge is speculative. Indeed, it is the end of the
knower that makes this knowledge speculative. If the
knower chose to make his science practical, then both
the science and the end of the knower would be purely
practical. But as the matter stands in the third
division, the science is only habitually or virtually
practical. Practical science, therefore, should be
placed in the fourth division.

II.   The Text from the De Veritate

     Will the examination of the parallel text, the De
Veritate 3,3[11] support the conclusions already drawn?
The text is as follows. Referring to the knowledge
that God has of His creatures, the question is: whether
ideas pertain to speculative or only to practical knowledge? Objection One states the basic difficulty.
Citing St. Augustine, it goes as follows:

          "Ideas are the principle forms of things
          according to which everything is formed that
          has a beginning or an end." But since nothing
          is formed by reason of speculative knowledge,
          ideas do not belong to this type of knowledge.[12]

---

ordination or non-ordination of the knowing subject to
a practical end. In other words, he is thinking of the
actual use which the subject makes of this knowledge,
and that depends upon the latter's free will and could
not enter the specification of his habitus (cf. Cajetan
In I, XIV, XVI; . . .)." The Degrees of Knowledge,
pp. 558-559. Thus because Maritain does not allow the
actual choice of the knower to enter into the specification of his habitus, he sees no difficulty in calling
the knowledge itself in the third division practical.

     [11]The translations of the texts from the De Ver.
3,3 in this section are taken from The Disputed Questions
of Truth, tr. by Robert Mulligan (Chicago, 1952), pp.
150-153.

     [12]Mulligan translates the phrase "formae rerum prin-
cipales" as "the principle forms of things." A sug-
gested translation is "the source forms of things."

The problem here is essentially the same as that treated in the article from the _Summa_. The objection is that, because God produces things by his knowledge of their forms, He cannot have speculative knowledge of these forms, for speculative knowledge does not result in the production of anything. But Thomas will argue that God has speculative knowledge of his productions.

Thomas proceeds to explain that there are four types of knowledge. Before explaining these types, however, he lays down the twofold distinction of the sciences taken from Aristotle.

As is said in _The Soul_, "Practical knowledge differs from speculative knowledge in its end." For the end of speculative knowledge is simply truth, but the end of practical knowledge, as we read in the _Metaphysics_, is action.

In the light of this teaching from Aristotle, Thomas states the first two types of knowledge:

> Now some knowledge is called practical
> because it is directed to a work. This
> happens in two ways. In the first way, it
> is directed in act--that is, when it is
> actually directed to a certain work, as the
> form is which an artist preconceives and
> intends to introduce into matter. This is
> called actual practical knowledge and is
> the form by which knowledge takes place.
> At other times, however, there is a type
> of knowledge that is capable of being
> ordered to an act, but this ordering is not
> actual. For example an artist thinks out
> a form for his work, knows how it can be
> made, yet does not intend to make it. This
> is practical knowledge, not actual, but
> habitual or virtual.

Are the two types of knowledge here equivalent to the third and fourth divisions mentioned in the _Summa_? The following text shows that they are.

> Since His knowledge causes things, He knows
> some things by ordaining by a decree of His
> will that they come into existence at a
> certain time. Of these things He has actual

practical knowledge. Moreover, He knows
other things which He never intends to
make, for He knows those things which
do not exist, have not existed, and never
will exist. . . . Of these things He has
actual knowledge, not acutally practical
knowledge, however, but merely virtually
practical.

Obviously, actual practical knowledge is equivalent
to purely or simply practical knowledge. And habitually
practical knowledge is equivalent to knowledge of the
operable which is speculative according to end. The
fact that God chooses to contemplate rather than to
create certain things presupposes that He has the
ability to create them. Thus this knowledge, thought
essentially speculative in nature, may be called
virtually or habitually practical. The same point holds
even more clearly for a human artist. While God does
not acquire his practical ability, the human artist does
Only after acquiring practical science in the realm of
the purely practical will the artist be able to have
virtually practical knowledge.

The other two types of knowledge are as follows:

At still other times, knowledge is utterly
incapable of being ordered to execution.
Such knowledge is purely speculative. This
also happens in two ways. First, the knowledge is about those things whose natures
are such that they cannot be produced by the
knowledge of the knower, as is true for
example, when we think about natural things.
Second, it may happen that the thing known
is something that is producible through
knowledge but is not considered as producible
. . . . This is the kind of knowledge a
craftsman has when he thinks about a house
by reflecting only on its genus, differences,
properties, and other things of this sort. . .

In contrast to the two previous types of knowledge,
which are directed either actually or virtually to
production, these last two "are utterly incapable of
being ordered to execution." They are "purely speculative." Though named differently, these two types
correspond to the two types of knowledge which are
called in the Summa "speculative only" and "speculative

44

according to manner." The basic teaching underlying both texts is that, even though there is a difference between the non-operable and the operable, this difference in the material does not take away from the fact that both types of knowledge are the objects of speculative science.

Clearly, this text provides no more basis for placing practical science in the category of the habitually practical than the text from the _Summa_ provided for placing practical science in the category of the operable speculatively considered according to end. The only category, then, in which one can place practical science is in that of the purely or actually practical.

III   The Text from the Commentary on the _De_ _Trinitate_

There remains one more text from St. Thomas which has a bearing on the views of the commentators. In his commentary on the _De_ _Trinitate_ of Boethius, Thomas asks the question: "Is speculative science appropriately divided into these three parts: the natural, the mathematical and the divine?"[13] Objection Four states:

> Medicine seems to be the most operative science, and yet it is said to contain a speculative part and a practical part. By the same token, therefore, all the other operative sciences have a speculative part. Consequently, even though it is a practical science, ethics or moral science should be mentioned in this division because of its speculative part.

The objection is quite clear. On the basis of the two-fold division of the sciences, the speculative sciences are metaphysics, mathematics and natural philosophy. Moral philosophy is classed with the practical sciences. Now the practical science of medicine is spoken of as having a speculative part, which deals with

---

[13]All of the translations of the text are from A. Maurer's _The_ _Division_ _and_ _Methods_ _of_ _the_ _Sciences_, Q.1, art.1.

principles remote from action, and a practical part, which deals with principles proximate to action. Since moral science is similar to medicine, should not its speculative part be listed with the speculative sciences?

St. Thomas' answer to Objection Four goes as follows:

> We divide philosophy with respect to the final end or happiness, to which the whole of human life is directed. . . And since the philosophers teach that there is a twofold happiness, one contemplative and the other active, as is clear in the Ethics /X,7-8, 1177a12ff/ they have accordingly also distinguished between two parts of philosophy, calling moral philosophy practical and natural . . . philosophy theoretical.

To divide philosophy in view of man's final end, happiness, is to divide it in the most fundamental way possible. The final end accounts for all of the operations of man. Since happiness itself consists primarily in the activity of acting, then the habits which perfect these activities are twofold. These are the speculative and practical sciences. On this basis medicine and morals are practical.

Yet medicine is said to have a speculative part. On what basis is this division made?

> When we divide medicine into theoretical and practical, the division is not on the basis of the end. For on that basis the whole of medicine is practical, since it is directed to practice. But the above division is made on the basis of whether what is studied in medicine is proximate to, or remote from practice. . . . Consequently, if we call some part of a practical science theoretical, we should not on that account place that part under speculative philosophy.

One may conclude, then, that if anyone possesses the art of medicine, he possesses the skill to use this art. Consequently, one who has the speculative part must also have this skill if his knowledge is truly practical.

But Maritain maintains that the expert in moral

philosophy (what he calls speculatively practical science) does not necessarily possess the virtue of prudence, which is the ability and willingness to act well. This stand of Maritain goes clearly against St. Thomas' notion of practical science. For even if moral science is divided into a theoretical and a practical part, the possessor of the theoretical part must possess both the required habituation and the intention of using that knowledge. If a man possesses the theory but not the ability to use it, he cannot be said to have practical science even habitually, let alone actually.

What Maritain calls speculatively practical science, then, is really speculative through and through according to the conception of St. Thomas. The fact that even a sinner can contemplate the truth about what actions accord with man's end does not mean that he is even remotely practical. For the notion of the practical implies seeking, not merely contemplating, man's good.

IV. Conclusion

This chapter has shown that in the three texts just analyzed--all of them dealing with the practical arts--St. Thomas is faithful to the radical distinction between speculative and practical science as laid down in his commentary on the Nicomachean Ethics. Since the object of practical science is the operable considered as operable, moral science must be simply practical in nature and method.

Consequently, the three texts examined above cannot be used to support the positions of the commentators, who maintain that the object of moral philosophy is some form of the operable speculatively considered. There seems to be little doubt, then, that the differences between the commentators and St. Thomas are quite deep. Given this difference in starting points, one would not be surprised to find differences in the nature and method of moral science or in the relationship of moral science to both prudence on the one extreme and the speculative sciences on the other.

Yet the argument so far has been based mainly on the radical distinction as found in the commentary on the Ethics and supported by the commentary on the

De <u>Trinitate</u>. It is time to look at the commentary on
the <u>Ethics</u> itself in order to determine St. Thomas'
conception of moral philosophy. Having seen the consequences that flow from the commentator's definition
of the object of moral science, the reader should be
in a position to compare them with the consequences
that St. Thomas draws out, not in comments scattered
throughout his works, but in a book whose whole purpose
is to define and then portray what moral philosophy is.

CHAPTER III

THE OBJECT OF MORAL SCIENCE IN
THE COMMENTARY ON THE ETHICS

The commentary includes an introductory statement
in which St. Thomas himself defines the object and
nature of moral philosophy. It also includes a line by
line analysis of the Ethics, in which Aristotle himself
defines the object, nature and method of moral science
in his own introduction and illustrates these notions
in the remaining ten books. An examination of the
commentary then should provide the answers to our
questions.

Of course, if St. Thomas had written a special
work portraying his own notion of moral philosophy, that
work would be a primary source for our investigation.
But Thomas wrote no such work. May the views of Thomas,
then, be found in his commentary on Aristotle? Certainly
there are problems about how one should interpret the
sententia or expositio of a medieval theologian whose
interest in Aristotle stems from a devotion to theology.
But the discussion of these problems, which has been
discussed elsewhere,[1] is beyond the scope of this book.
Nevertheless one may at least assume at the outset
that for St. Thomas the problem about the object of
moral philosophy is a matter, not just of what Aristotle
says, but of truth. Consequently, if St. Thomas has
any disagreements with Aristotle, one may expect St.
Thomas to indicate those disagreements in some way.[2]

Following the order of the commentary, this chapter
will discuss problems relating to the object of moral
philosophy by examining 1) the introduction of St. Thomas

---

[1]See Joseph Owens, "Aquinas as Aristotelian Com-
mentator" St. Thomas Aquinas 1274-1974 Commemorative
Studies, (Toronto: Pontifical Institute of Mediaeval
Studies, 1974) p.213-238.

[2]As a matter of fact, one cannot often find St.
Thomas flatly disagreeing with Aristotle. One instance
does come to mind (VI,1,150). But the disagreement
arises, not from any clash between the general views of
St. Thomas and Aristotle, but from an apparent incon-
sistency in the views of Aristotle himself. For the

himself and 2) his commentary on the introduction of
Aristotle. The object and nature of moral science
having been determined, chapter four will discuss the
relationship of moral science to both the arts and
metaphysics. Chapter five will discuss the method of
moral science in contrast to that of speculative science.
Chapter six will summarize the main conclusions.

I   The Introduction of St. Thomas

    The introduction of Thomas may be divided into
three parts. In the first part (I,1,1-14) he determines
the object. In the second part (15-54) he determines
the science that treats of this object. In the third
part (55-106) St. Thomas, drawing upon Christian rather
than ancient Greek culture, divides moral philosophy
itself. This division will be discussed in chapter
four while the first two parts will be treated now.

    St. Thomas, very first words declare the role that
he will take in the introduction. "As the Philosopher
says in the beginning of the Metaphysics, it is the
role of the wise man to put things in order. For wisdom is the greatest perfection of reason, whose proper
function is to know order . . . ."[3] Here St. Thomas
assumes the role of the metaphysician, not of the moral
philosopher. Why? The reason is that he intends to
define the object of moral philosophy. Now to define
anything is to situate it in relationship to all other
things by showing how it is both like and unlike them.
Since only the metaphysician knows the whole order of

---

most part, however, St. Thomas is content to interpret
the text as it stands. One cannot take this procedure
to mean that St. Thomas is in total agreement with
Aristotle. For in his introduction, St. Thomas has already defined moral philosophy in a Christian setting
rather than in the Greek setting of Aristotle. This
point will be discussed in detail in chapter four pp.

[3]"Sicut Philosophus dicit in principio Metaphysicae,
sapientis est ordinare. Cuius ratio est quia sapientia
est potissima perfectio rationis, quia proprium est
cognoscere ordinem . . . " (I,1,1-4). Because there is
not yet a recognized translation from the new edition
of the Sententia Ethicorum, the latin will be given
below for each quotation above.

reality, only he can define the relationship of things to each other within that order. And since reality specifies science, it follows that only the metaphysician knows the relationship of the sciences to each other.

The moral philosopher, on the other hand, is a competent judge only in his own order. While he knows his own object in a certain way, he cannot define it, for the knowledge of its definition is a perfect kind of knowledge which he can acquire only with the help of the metaphysician.

The text has already indicated one relationship that the metaphysician has to moral philosophy and, indeed, to all the sciences. He can consider any science as an object of contemplation in order to grasp the necessities involved in that object. This contemplative exercise does not make the other science part of or subalternate to metaphysics. While it is true that the material of metaphysics includes that of all the other sciences, still metaphysics considers all beings from the aspect of their existence. The objects of the other sciences are beings considered in some other way. Since each science has its own object, it has its own autonomy and identity. Such is the Aristotelian and Thomistic conception of the sciences.

The process of definition begins with Thomas standing before reality and the ways of knowing it. Starting with this whole, he will mark off in successively narrowing terms the object of moral science. His first step is to mark off the object of reason from that of the sense powers: "even if the sensible powers know something absolutely, nevertheless to know the order of one thing to another is exclusively the work of intellect or reason."[4]

Thus Thomas indicates that reality provides the material for two ways of knowing it. One way is through the sense powers, whose object is something absolute; i.e., sensible things or human operations, both known

---

[4] ". . . etsi vires sensitivae cognoscant res aliquas absolute, ordinem tamen unius rei ad aliam cognoscere est solius intellectus aut rationis." Sent. Ethic. I,1,4-7.

in their particularity. The other way is through reason, which knows the order of one thing to another; i.e., the relationship of effect to cause or of cause to effect.[5]

While these two objects are distinct, they are also closely related. This point may be illustrated by reviewing the ways that man knows the world.[6] The world consists of individual entities. Initially, man either knows or causes them through particular reason, which is directly dependent upon the information supplied by the sense powers. After repeated exercises of particular reason,[7] man acquires what is technically known as experience,[7] which may be either speculative or practical.

Experience in speculative matters enables man to recognize the recurring connections between one thing and another, the patterns in events. He notes, for example, men and their ability to speak. He knows that this connection must have a cause because it is not haphazard. However, he does not yet know the cause itself.

Experience in practical matters enables man to operate well by imparting both the skills and knowledge

---

[5] "For to proceed from causes to effects or the reverse is not an activity of the senses but only of the intellect." St. Thomas Aquinas, Commentary on the Metaphysics of Aristotle, trans. by J. Rowan, (Chicago, 1961) vol. II, Bk. VI, lect. 1, no. 1146, p. 457.

[6] In his Commentary on the Metaphysics of Aristotle, Bk. I, lect. 1, no. 5-35, pp. 8-16, St. Thomas gives an extended treatment of the knowledge of man. He starts with the knowledge of the sense powers, which man has in common with the animals, and moves on through various stages until he arrives at scientific knowledge, which is proper to man alone.

[7] "For an experience arises from the association of many singular (intentions) received in memory. And this kind of association is proper to man, and pertains to the cogitative power (also called particular reason), which associates particular intentions just as universal reason associates universal ones." Ibid., Bk. I, lect. 1, no.15, p.11.

that come from long involvement in practical affairs.
For example, the experienced man will be able to cure
a sickness by using herbs. While experience, however,
knows the connection in fact between a particular
course of action and a particular effect, it does not
know the cause of the connection.

Universal reason enters the scene when man discovers the cause or reason for the fact. When the
spectator grasps, for example, that this man is a
rational animal, he knows then why the man has the
ability to speak. Having grasped the universal in the
particular, he then knows why all men must have this
ability unless, of course, something interferes with
the nature of some. Again, when the agent, for example,
knows the particular property which enables a certain
herb to cure sickness, he knows the cause. Hence, he
knows why all herbs of a certain type cure certain
types of sickness.

It is clear, then, why the objects of experience
and of reason are distinct and yet related. They are
distinct because knowing the particular as such is
not necessarily grasping the universal in the particular. Knowing the fact is not necessarily knowing the
reasoned fact. Yet they are related because one cannot
grasp the universal in the particular unless he first
knows the particular. In brief, without experience
there is no science.

Thomas proceeds to explain in more detail the
object of universal reason, thus putting aside the
object of experience:

> A twofold order is found in things: one
> kind is that of the parts of any whole or
> any multitude to each other, as the parts
> of a house are ordered to each other. The
> other kind is the order of things to a goal.
> This order is more important than the first.
> For, as the Philosopher says in the Meta-
> physics, the order of the parts of an army
> to each other is due to the order of the
> whole army to the leader.[8]

---

[8]"Invenitur autem duplex ordo in rebus: unus quidem
partium alicuius totius seu alicuius multitudinis ad
invicem, sicut partes domus ad invicem ordinantur;

The order of a whole to its goal is more important
than the order of the parts in that whole to each other.
For the order within the whole is the effect of which
the goal is the final cause. To understand the whole,
therefore, universal reason seeks to know the cause.

Obviously, the order of the non-operable already
exists before the man of science fully grasps it. Less
obvious but nevertheless true is the fact that the
order of the operable also exists before the man of
practical science grasps it. For man by means of productive experience and prudence has established a
human order long before the spectator contemplates it
for the sake of truth or the practical scientist understands it for the sake of action.

Thomas proceeds to designate the four orders or
objects of universal reason:

> Order is related to reason in a fourfold
> way. There is an order which reason does
> not establish but only considers, such as the
> things in nature. There is another order
> which reason establishes among its own acts
> by its considerations, as when it orders its
> concepts to each other and also the signs
> of concepts, which are words. Third, there
> is the order which reason establishes among
> the operations of the will by its considera-
> tions. Fourth, there is the order which reason
> establishes among exterior things by its con-
> siderations, things of which it is the cause,
> as a chest or a house.[9]

---

alius autem est ordo rerum in finem, et hic ordo est
principalior quam prius, nam, ut Philosophus dicit in
. . . Metaphysicae, ordo partium exercitus ad invicem
est propter ordinem totius exercitus ad ducem" Sent.
Ethic. I,1,7-14.

[9]"Ordo autem quadrupliciter ad rationem comparatur:
est enim quidem ordo quem ratio non facit, sed solum
considerat, sicut est ordo rerum naturalium; alius autem
est ordo quem ratio considerando facit in proprio actu,
puta cum ordinat conceptus suos ad invicem et signa
conceptuum, quae sunt voces significativae; tertius
autem est ordo quem ratio considerando facit in operationibus voluntatis; quartus autem est ordo quem ratio
considerando facit in exterioribus rebus quorum ipsa

It has already been explained how these four objects of science may be reduced to two, the speculative and the practical, and how moral science is defined in the light of this radical distinction. But before proceeding to examine the Aristotelian background of these texts, let us pause for a moment to explore the implications of the radical distinction. Taking the two generic objects, we will deduce the necessities that flow from them. Although the task of this and the suceeding chapters will be to trace this deduction in the texts, an outline here of the basic argument should be helpful.

First, when the object of reason is any reality (human operations included) considered simply for the sake of truth, this reality must be already established. Otherwise, there will be no actuality present to rule or measure the spectator's reason.[10] These actualities, then, are the starting points or foundations or first principles of reason's activities. They dictate all that reason will say about them. Thus they serve as the standard[11] inwhose light reason is judged to speak the truth or not.

On the other hand, when the object of reason is the establishment of human operations in due order, these entities are things to be established. Consequently, these future operations cannot be the rule or measure of reason. Rather reason is their rule or measure.[12] Since actions to be done must be in accord with reason and reason must be in accord with right desire, the standard of practical truth resides within man himself.[13] Hence the starting points or foundations

---

est causa, sicut in arca et domo" Sent. Ethic. I,1,14-24.

[10]See below, p. 55, note 12.

[11]See below, p. 106, note 30.

[12]"Note, however, that a thing is referred differently to the practical intellect than it is to the speculative intellect. Since the practical intellect causes things, it is a measure of what it causes. But, since the speculative intellect is receptive in regard to things, it is, in a certain sense, moved by things and consequently measured by them." St. Thomas Aquinas, The Disputed Questions of Truth, 1,2c, p.11.

[13]See below, chapter five, p. 110, note 38.

or first principles of all practical considerations are found ultimately in human choice, the efficient cause which establishes human order in view of a final cause which itself is a human operation conceived as a goal.[14]

Second, for the spectator to attain the truth about the object he contemplated, he must have had prior experience of the facts. If he does not know the fact, how can he discover the cause of the fact?

On the other hand, for the agent to attain the universal truth to be used for the sake of action, he must already have had the practical experience which comes from personal involvement in the affairs of life. Otherwise he can have no basis upon which to reflect and no ability to act upon these reflections.[15]

Third, to attain the truth in speculative science the spectator must reason analytically, i.e., from effect to cause. For experience of the facts supplies the effects which universal reason must analyze to discover the causes.

On the other hand, for the agent to attain the goal of action, he must reason synthetically, i.e., from cause to effect. The effect he seeks to enact is some particular product or deed.[16] Thus he must start his reasoning from universal norms, which are a kind of exemplary cause. Of course, to possess these norms in a fully explicit way, he must already have derived them from experience.

Fourth, for the spectator to attain the truth, his

---

[14]See below, p. 73.

[15]See below, chapter five, pp. 124-126.

[16]". . . considerandum est quod in speculativis scientiis, in quibus non quaeritur nisi cognitio veritatis, sufficit cognoscere quae sit causa talis effectus; sed in scientiis operativis, quorum finis est operatio, oportet cognoscere qualibus motibus seu operationibus talis effectus a tali causa sequatur" Sent. Ethic. II, 2,16-21.

object must be necessary or unchanging.[17] While the
particulars he starts with are certainly contingent,
they are considered for the sake of the necessities involved in their existence.[18] These necessities are
their various causes. Thus, facts explained in terms
of their causes constitute an object which cannot be
otherwise. Since this object is the same for all spectators independently of their own particular opinions
or desires, it is strictly objective. The only role
that man's will plays in this knowing is to turn the
intellect towards the truth.

On the other hand, because the goal of practical
science is to serve as an aid in the establishment of
some deed or product, its object is variable or contingent.[19] Here human operations, which are contingent,
are considered in their very contingency.[20] For the
nature and existence of any operation depends upon how

---

[17]". . . una quidem, quae speculatur necessaria,
potest dici scientificum genus animae, quia scientia de
necessariis est. . ." Sent. Ethic., VI,1,138-140.

[18]"Universales quidem igitur rationes contingentium
immutabiles sunt, et secundum hoc de his demonstrationes
dantur et ad scientias demonstrativas pertinet eorum
cognitio; non enim scientia naturalis est solum de
rebus necessariis et incorruptibilibus, sed etiam de
rebus corruptibilibus et contingentibus. . ." Sent.
Ethic., VI,1,194-200.

[19]". . . alia autem pars potest dici rationativa,
secundum quod rationcinari et consiliari pro eodem sumitur nominat; enim consilium quandam inquisitionem nondum
determinatam, sicut et rationcinatio, quae quidem inde-
terminatio maxime accidit circa contingentia, de quibus solis est consilium, nullus enim consiliatur de his
quae non contingit aliter se habere" Sent. Ethic., VI,1
141-147.

[20]"Alio modo possunt accipi contingentia secundum
quod sunt in particulari, et sic variabilia sunt nec
cadit supra ea intellectus nisi mediantibus potentiis
sensitivis; unde et inter partes animae sensitivas ponitur
una potentia quae dicitur ratio particularis sive vis
cogitativa, quae est collativa intentionum particularium;
sic autem accipit his Philosophus contingentia, ita enim
cadunt sub consilio et operatione. . ." Sent. Ethic.,
VI,1,203-211.

the agent judges the various circumstances in which he finds himself. Certainly the agent exercises a consistency in judgment due to his proper orientation towards his proper good, an orientation articulated in universal norms. But these norms are flexible because they include only in an indeterminate way the infinite number of means that man has of attaining his goal. These norms, then, are neither objective nor subjective. They are not objective because they are the flexible measures guiding the implementation of man's desire,[21] not the fixed measure resulting from reason being measured by a necessary object. Nor are they subjective because they are, after all, universal and so are for all men.

Fifth, when the spectator attains the unchanging truth about his object, he can rest in the fully rounded or perfect certitude of his attainment.[22] Knowing the necessity of his reasoning, he knows that his conclusions cannot be otherwise.

On the other hand, because the goal of practical science is to aid the agent in operating well, practical certitude is not primarily concerned with the correctness of its universal norms but with the rightness of particular operations. Of course, the agent does have full certainty about the general truth of his norms. Yet this certainty should not be considered perfect or fully rounded because universal norms of action are indefinite in regard to the particular.[23] Hence to be certain about the norm itself is not to be certain about the particular.

In conclusion, when things are considered simply for the sake of truth, they constitute an unchanging object of speculative science, which reasons analytically and thereby attains perfect certitude. On the other hand, when human operations are considered for the sake of action, they constitute a variable object of practical science, which reasons synthetically and thereby attains practical certitude.

***

---

[21]See below, chapter five, p. 106.

[22]See below, chapter five, pp. 103-104.

[23]See below, chapter five, p. 99, note 17; p. 100, note 19.

There seems to be no doubt that moral philosophy
is an intellectual virtue which is practical. Yet
Aristotle does not mention moral science in his classification of the five intellectual virtues.[24] Nor does
Thomas mention it in his commentary on this passage.[25]
He mentions wisdom, science and understanding (the
speculative intellectual virtues); art and prudence,
(the practical intellectual virtues). How can the
apparent omission of moral science from the list of the
intellectual virtues be explained?

The answer is to be found in the analysis of the
following text:

> And although moral science is directed to
> action, still that action is not the act
> of the science but rather of virtue, as is
> clear in the Ethics. So we cannot call
> moral science art; but rather in these actions
> virtue takes the place of art.[26]

Although moral science is for the sake of operation,
the operation itself is not the act of science but of
virtue. In other words the activity of the moral
philosopher, while it is directed to action, is not the
same as the activity of the virtuous man, which is
identical with good action. This is so because moral
science is a solely intellectual virtue[27] whose function
is to help in reasoning from the universal to the particular. But the great impediment to correct moral
reasoning is not purely intellectual. Rather it is a
disordered character, which especially corrupts one's

---

[24]E.N. VI,3,1139b16-17.

[25]"Sunt autem quinque numero quibus anima semper
dicit verum vel affirmando vel negando, scilicet ars,
scientia, prudentia, sapientia et intellectus" Sent.
Ethic., VI,3,16-19.

[26]In Boeth. de Trin., V,1,ad 3, A. Maurer's
translation.

[27]That moral science is solely an intellectual
virtue is clear from the following, where St. Thomas
contrasts the intellectual virtues of prudence and of
moral science: ". . . in quantum enim sunt in sola
ratione, dicuntur quaedam scientiae practicae, scilicet
ethica, yconomica et politica" Sent. Ethic., VI,7,93-95.

judgment of the particular.[28] Consequently there is a need for an intellectual virtue which not only perfects reason but the appetites (will and passions) as well. This intellectual virtue is prudence.[29] Since prudence immediately controls particular choice, an act of prudence is identical with a good act.

A good act, however, is only indirectly an act of moral science. For the man of moral science does not reason correctly from the universal to the particular simply on the strength of his knowledge of universal norms. He needs prudence in order to terminate successfully the reasoning process. Furthermore, a good act is not simply the product of reason, either universal or particular. It is the product of choice, which is an act of particular reason and the will.[30] Since prudence perfects choice, the moral philosopher must be prudent to attain the goal of his science.

But in the realm of production only intellectual perfection is required.[31] For the technical perfection

[28]". . . quando autem est vehemens delectatio vel tristitia, apparet homini quod illud sit optimum per quod sequitur delectationem et fugit tristitiom, et ita, corrupto iudicio rationis, non apparet homini verus finis, qui est principium prudentiae circa operabilia existentis. . ." Sent. Ethic., VI,4,131-136.

[29]". . . patet quod prudentia non est ars, quasi in sola veritate rationis constituens, sed est virtus ad modum moralium virtutum requirens rectitudinem appetitus" Sent. Ethic., VI,4,174-177.

[30]". . . electio est appetitus consiliativus, sequitur quod sit actus principium unde motus, id est per modum causae efficientis. . ." Sent. Ethic., VI,2, 149-151.

[31]The following texts from Aristotle and St. Thomas show how the intellect, which has a major part in the acquisition of the speculative sciences and the productive arts, has a relatively small role in the acquisition of moral virtue or prudence. Aristotle says: " . . . but as a condition of the possession of the virtues knowledge has little or no weight, while the other conditions count not for a little but for everything, i.e., the very conditions which result from often doing just and temperate acts" (E.N. II,4,1105b2-4) St. Thomas comments: ". . . sed scientia parvam vel

of a work or product does not depend upon the moral
character of the agent but simply upon his practical
intelligence. Master criminals and mad scientists are
cases in point. In matters of production, then, art
controls the reasoning from the universal to the particular. And since art is a more powerful intellectual
instrument than experience alone, the perfect act of
production is attributed to art rather than to experience.

Because the act of production is identical with the
activity of art and good actions are identical with the
activity of prudence, Aristotle and Thomas list these
as the intellectual virtues of practical reason. These
virtues are immediately concerned with the practical
goal of enacting some deed or product. Moral science
is not listed because its activity is not identical with
the act towards which it is directed. Nevertheless,
as the texts will show later,[32] moral science is derived
from the experience of the prudent man for the purposes
of the prudent man. Thus one should not be tempted to
list moral science under the category of the intellecual
virtue of science, which is speculative in nature.

Before concluding this section on St. Thomas' own
introduction to his commentary on the Ethics, two points
are to be noted about the background from which Thomas
derives his teaching. The first concerns the source in
Aristotle for Thomas' way of dividing practical from
speculative science. And the second concerns the source
in Aristotle for Thomas' way of starting with the object
in his definition of science.

Concerning the first point, the basic pattern upon
which the introduction of St. Thomas is based may be
found in the following text of Aristotle:

And since natural science, like other

----

nullam virtutem habet ad hoc quod homo sit virtuosus,
sed totum consistit in aliis, quae quidem adveniunt
homini ex frequenti operatione virtuosum operum, quia
ex hoc generatur habitus per quem aliquis eligit ea quae
conveniunt illi habitui et immobiliter in eis perseverat"
Sent. Ethic., II,4,80-86.

[32] See below, pp. 126-127.

sciences, is in fact about one class of
being, i.e. of that sort of substance which
has the principles of its movement and rest
present in itself, evidently it is neither
practical nor productive. For in the case
of things made the principle is in the
maker--it is either reason or art or some
faculty, while in the case of things done
it is in the doer--viz. will, for that
which is done and that which is willed are
the same (<u>Metaphy</u>. VI,1,1025b19-28).[33]

Here Aristotle is concerned with distinguishing the
speculative science of natural philosophy from the
practical sciences. He distinguishes between the two
on the basis of their objects. The object of natural
science is the truth about natural substances, which
have a principle of motion and rest within them. The
material is not that of either the practical (moral) or
the productive sciences. For the material of the latter
is either some product or some action, both caused by
man himself.

At this point the radical difference between the
materials of natural science and of the others is obvious. But a difference in objects is not determined
simply by a difference in material. Only when one
treats matters of choice or of production for the sake
of choosing or producing does one have an object which
is radically distinct from the object of the speculative
sciences.

The basic difference, then, between the speculative
and practical sciences is ultimately due to the fact
that man alone of all terrestrial creatures has the
power of choice. Thus he is not determined in his
actions in the way that all other natural things are.
Rather he has the power to determine his own acts.
Consequently he alone can set up a science whose goal
is to establish a human order, which does not exist by
nature and need not even exist by man unless he so
chooses.

---

[33]Concerning this passage, Joseph Owens says: "It
can be safely taken as giving Aristotle's mature conception of the sciences." "The Grounds of Ethical
Universality in Aristotle," <u>Man and World</u>, 2(1969), p.
174.

Concerning the second point, the order of St. Thomas' exposition: the basic reason why Thomas begins with the definition of the object of science may be found in the following text of Aristotle:

> But if we are to express what each is, viz.
> what the thinking power is, or the perceptual,
> or the nutritive, we must go farther back
> and first give an account of thinking or
> perceiving, for in the order of investiga-
> tion the question of what an agent does pre-
> cedes the question, what enables it to do
> what it does. If this is correct, we must
> on the same ground go yet another step
> farther back and have some clear view of
> the objects of each; thus we must start with
> these objects, e.g. with food, with what
> is perceptible, or with what is intelligible"
> (De An. II,4,415a15-23).

According to Aristotle if one wishes to define a thinking power, he must do so in terms of the activity of that power, which is thinking. But in order to de- fine thinking, one must know what the thinking is about, i.e., the intelligible. In brief, to define the nature of a thinking power one must define its object. For a power is a potentiality which can be understood only in terms of something actual. As St. Thomas says in his commentary on this passage:

> Potentiality is nothing but a capacity to
> act or be acted upon; it essentially involves
> a relation to actuality and can only be de-
> fined in such terms. And if this is the case
> with acts and potencies, acts in their turn
> connote something prior to themselves, i.e.,
> their objects. For the type of every act
> or operation is determined by the object.[34]

Thus all powers and their activities are defined in terms of their objects. Since reason is an active power, its object is also its final goal. For "the objects of active capacities are related to these as the final terms attained by their activities; for in

---

[34]St. Thomas Aquinas, De Anima, trans. by K. Foster et al. (New Haven, 1951), Bk. II, lect.6, no.304, p.78.

this case the object is what each of these activities effectively realizes."[35]

Because science is a habit perfecting the power of reason, science is also defined in terms of its object. The object in this case is either all of reality considered simply for the sake of truth or human actions considered for the sake of action. These objects, then, are highly complex, having within them both what is known immediately and what is known after reasoning. In short, the object fully understood is the whole science. But the whole science must already include the method by which it is known. Thus in the very act of determining the object of a science one also determines its method.

If, however, one introduces a real distinction between the object of a science and either its end or method (mode), one has broken the necessary connection between the object and the method of a science. To that extent one's notion of a science is neither Aristotelian nor Thomistic.

It is clear, then, that the most important step in any discussion about the nature and method of a science is the definition of its object.

II. Thomas' Commentary on the Introduction of Aristotle

The issue to be investigated in this section is again the question of what constitutes the object of moral science. Since the basic position argued for here is, to judge by the prevailing opinions on the matter, novel, an elaborate examination of the text seems appropriate. Thus if all the elements in the text support our interpretation, it should gain in credibility.

Are the first three chapters of Book One of the Ethics really Aristotle's introduction to moral science? The answer is yes according to St. Thomas.

> Aristotle, beginning to treat the first part
> of moral philosophy in this book which is
> called the Ethics, that is, Morals, presents

---

[35]Ibid., Bk. II, lect. 6, no.305, p.78.

an introduction in which he does three
things: first, he shows what his intention
is; second, he shows the method of treating
it . . .; third, he shows the kind of learner
one must have for this science . . . .[36]

Calling the Ethics the first part of moral philosophy,[37] Thomas notes that Aristotle divides the first
three chapters of Book One into three parts. In the
first part (the first two chapters) Aristotle defines
the object and nature of ethics. In the second part
(the first half of chapter three) he defines its method.
In the third part (the last half of chapter three) he
describes the learner. This section will examine the
comments of Thomas upon the first part.

As the analysis of the text will show, the introductory argument is speculative in nature. Can one say
it is, like St. Thomas' own introduction, metaphysical?
Since the speculative sciences are natural philosophy,
mathematics and metaphysics, and since the opening
argument is obviously not mathematical, the other al-
ternative is to call the argument one of natural philosophy. Is the argument, then, physical or metaphysical?
The answer to this question may be found in Aristotle's
De Anima and in St. Thomas' commentary on that work.
Aristotle, seeking the nature of the science which
treats of the operations of the soul, says: "If there
is any way of acting or being acted upon proper to the
soul, soul will be capable of separate existence; if
there is none, its separate existence is impossible."[38]
In the first case the study of the operations of the
soul will be conducted by "the First Philosopher or

------

[36]"Incipiens igitur Aristotiles tradere moralem
philosophiam a prima sui parte in hoc libro qui dicitur
Ethicorum, id est Moralium, praemittit prooemium, in
quo tria facit: primo enim ostendit de quo est intentio;
secundo modum tractandi . . .; tertio qualis debeat
esse auditor scientiae . . ." Sent. Ethic., I,1,107-113.

[37]The first part deals with the individual. The
other two parts are domestic and political (I,1,100-
106). The significance of this division, which is not
Aristotelian, will be discussed in chapter four.

[38]De Anima I,1,403a11-12.

metaphysician".[39] In the second case the study is
proper to the natural philosopher.

The commentary of Thomas shows that he accepts
Aristotle's position.[40] Consequently Thomas, using the
criterion of Aristotle, would hold that the introductory
argument is metaphysical. For the argument is, as we
shall see, about man's highest good. This good is a
contemplative operation proper to the soul alone. Since
the soul can exist apart from the body, it is discussed
in metaphysics, which treats of substances which either
can or do exist apart from a body.

Aristotle begins his project of defining the object
of moral philosophy by stating: "Every art and every
inquiry, and similarly every action and pursuit, is
thought to aim at some good . . . ."[41] St. Thomas,
citing the De Anima, explains the terms of this proposition: "there are two principles of human acts;
namely, intellect or reason and appetite, which are the
principles of movement. . . ."[42] The principle of
reason, which is divided into speculative and practical,
results in science (inquiry) and art. The principle of
appetite or will results in the operations of choice
(pursuit) and action. The feature common to all of
these operations is that they are performed for the
sake of some goal. For example, the goal of scientific
operations is to attain the truth, which is one type of
good. The goal of the operations of art is to make
some work or product, which is another type of good.
And the goal of the operations of choice is to choose
or act, which is still another type of good.

The brevity of Aristotle's opening statement and
the analytic nature of Thomas' comments should not
blind the reader to the factual basis upon which the
whole inquiry into the object of moral science begins.
The facts are when this or that man acts, he has this

---

[39]De Anima I,1,403b16.

[40]In . . . De Anima Bk.I, lect.2, no.20 and 28.

[41]E.N. I,1,1094a1-2.

[42]" . . . duo sunt principia humanorum actuum,
scilicet intellectus seu ratio et appetitus, quae sunt
principia moventia . . ." Sent. Ethic., I,1,128-131.

goal or that purpose in mind. Further observation of particular cases shows the same connection between human acts on the one hand and goals on the other. Yet the evidence of particular cases, even if there are millions of them, does not by itself allow the universal conclusion that all human acts must be done for the sake of some goal (good). Before such a conclusion can be drawn one must see that the pursuit of goals is the basic reason why operations take place. When one has this insight into the cause of any particular action, he is then entitled to claim that, whenever a man acts as a man, he must act for the sake of some goal.

But the argument is moving ahead of itself. At this point the reader may make the claim that human operations seek some good simply as a matter of observed fact. To be shown is why this fact is necessarily so. Aristotle proceeds to show this by defining the notion of good: "The good has rightly been declared to be that at which all things aim."[43]

Thomas comments upon this last proposition, thereby embarking upon an elaborate definition of the notion of good.

> When he says: 'therefore they have spoken well etc.', he makes evident the truth of the previous proposition by defining the notion of good. Concerning this definition, it should be noted that good is counted among the first things . . . According to the truth of the matter, good is convertible with being. Now first things cannot be known through anything prior to them, just as causes are known through their own effects. Since good is properly the mover of appetite, then good is described through a motion of appetite, just as the moving power is ordinarily manifested through motion. For this reason he says that the philosophers have rightly declared that good is what all seek.[44]

---

[43]E.N. I,1,1094a23. Aristotle later attributes this definition to Eudoxus (E.N. X,2,1172b9).

[44]"Deinde cum dicit: 'Ideo bene enuntiaverunt etc.' manifestat propositum per diffinitionem boni. Circa quod considerandum est quod bonum numeratur inter prima

St. Thomas considers that the function of
Aristotle's definition of good is to show why the previous proposition--that all human operations aim at
some good--is necessarily true. Then Thomas proceeds
to define the notion of good by showing how it is both
like and unlike that most fundamental of all notions
and that most fundamental feature of any existent--
being.

He notes that "good is counted among the first
things". In other words, it is a basic cause. Furthermore, "good is convertible with being"; i.e., any good
insofar as it is a good is a being and any being insofar as it is a being is a good. Since being is predicated of all the categories of substance and accident
and of a primary cause beyond the categories, so too is
good predicated of all the categories and of a primary
cause beyond them. This conclusion follows from the
fact that there is a real identity between being and
good.

Next, St. Thomas makes the epistemological observation that first causes are known only through effects.
This observation is so because, since the knowledge of
man starts from sense experience, he is always aware of
effects before he discovers their causes. The truth of
this observation may be seen from the following. The
first cause of all being--being itself--is known only
through a demonstration which proceeds from an immediate
knowledge of sensible beings, which are effects. Again,
the first cause within the categories, substantial form,
is known only through its union with matter, this composition being an effect. And substantial beings themselves, which are the causes of accidental beings, are
known only through those accidental beings. Thus on all
levels the generalization holds that causes are known
only through their effects.

Since good is also a type of first cause, it too
is known only through its effects. But because the

. . . secundum rei veritatem bonum cum ente convertitur.
Prima autem non possunt notificari per aliqua priora,
sed notificantur per posteriora, sicut causae per pro-
prios effectus. Cum autem bonum proprie sit motivum
appetitus, describitur bonum per motum appetitus, sicut
solet manifestari vis motiva per motum. Et ideo dicit
quod philosophi bene enuntiaverunt bonum esse id quod
omnia appetunt" Sent. Ethic., I,1,148-160.

notion of good is logically, though not really, distinct
from being, it is a particular type of cause which is
known through its own type of effect. For the notion
of good, unlike that of being, always carries within
itself the aspect of relation to something else. That
something else is appetite, of which good "is properly
the mover". In other words, any good is a being
which is seen as the end or completion or perfection or
goal towards which the desire or appetite or operation
or tendency of another being moves. For example, when
one considers the separate and subsistent being as a
good, it is the final goal or reason why all things in
the universe move. Again, when one considers a material
substance as a good, it is the perfection that results
from the union of form and matter. Finally, when one
sees accidental form as a good, it is the being which
completes a substance; it is the goal towards which the
operations of a substance tend.

Since any good is a final cause or goal which is
known only through its effects, St. Thomas considers
the definition used by Aristotle to be appropriate.
For in describing good as that which all things seek,
Aristotle has described the cause in terms of its
effects.

So far Thomas' definition of good has shown that
it is a cause whose nature is final, not material,
efficient or formal. Thus from the fact that human
operations exist, one knows that human good must exist.
Without human goods, there could be no operations.
Thomas has also made an epistemological observation
which determines the method to be used in trying to
understand human goods. Because goods are known only
through their effects, one must begin his search for
human goods by analyzing their effects, human operations.

Up to this point Thomas has shown what human goods
have in common with good in general. He will next
distinguish human goods from all the other types of
good. Since the general notion of good can refer either
to the goods within the categories of being or to the
separate good beyond the categories, the question
naturally arises: to which class of goods do the goals
of human operation belong?

St. Thomas answers:

> It is not one good to which all things
> tend . . . and therefore some one good is

not being described here. Rather it is to
be understood as good in general. But
because nothing is good except insofar as
it is a certain likeness and a participa-
tion in the highest good, this highest good
itself is desired in a certain way when any
good is desired. In this way one can say
that the one good is what all things desire.[45]

The good to which all things tend is not the one
good of the whole universe but either the substantial
or the accidental goods within the categories. But
because things in seeking their own good also seek the
good beyond the categories, one may claim that all seek
the one separate good.

So far, then, it is clear that human goods are
within the categories. But are these goods within the
category of substance or of accident? Thomas answers:

the final good to which the appetite of
everything tends is its ultimate perfection.
The first perfection is in the manner of form
and the second perfection is in the manner
of operation.[46]

The final good sought by composite substances is
their ultimate perfection, which comes to them through
their operations. These final goods, then, are second
forms and so are in the category of accidents. They
are not first or substantial forms, which, in making
the substances exist, make them good.

The fact that man is a substance of a certain kind

---

[45]"Non autem est unum bonum in quod omnia tendunt
. . . et ideo non describitur hic aliquod unum bonum,
sed bonum describitur communiter sumptum; quia autem
nihil est bonum nisi in quantum est quaedam similitudo
et participatio summi boni, ipsum summum bonum quodam
modo appetitur in quolibet bono et sic potest dici
quod unum bonum est quod omnia appetunt" Sent. Ethic.,
I,1,175-183.
[46]" . . . finale bonum in quod tendit appetitus
uniuscuiusque est ultima perfectio eius. Prima autem
perfectio se habet per modum formae, secunda autem per
modum operationis" Sent. Ethic., I,1,186-189.

means that he has a natural capacity for perfection, which may be actualized by operations. When he acts, therefore, he must act by his very nature to realize some good. Otherwise he would not act at all. Yet experience shows that men do evil deeds for the sake of evil goals. How is this possible? Thomas answers:

> There is no problem about the fact that some men seek evil. For they seek evil only under the aspect of good insofar as they consider it good. Hence their intention primarily aims at good and only incidentally touches on evil.[47]

St. Thomas admits that some men seek evil. But since an evil end is still a goal, it must be some kind of good. Otherwise there would be no reason at all why a man should do evil. Consequently the proposition holds that, no matter what any man does, he does it for the sake of some good.

That man can pursue evil indicates his difference from non-rational agents. The latter seek and for the most part attain their proper good by operations flowing from their nature by necessity. But man, while he has a proper good by nature, does not necessarily act for its sake. Having the power of choice, he may choose, not his real, but only his apparent good. Because of this power, one may then speak of moral good or evil.

Here the examination of Thomas' commentary on the first two propositions of Aristotle's ends. Starting with the general notion of good, Thomas has narrowed down that notion until he has shown that man has natural goals or goods which he may attain by the power of choice. What remains to be shown is that, given the fact that man has natural goals, there must be some highest goal which is the final cause of all the others. If such a highest goal exists, one may then begin an inquiry into its nature so that, in understanding the highest cause, one will then understand its effects.

Because effects must be understood in terms of

---

[47]"Nec est instantia de quibusdam qui appetunt malum, quia non appetunt malum nisi sub ratione boni, in quantum scilicet aestimant illud esse bonum, et sic intentio eorum per se fertur ad bonum, sed per accidens

their cause, Aristotle begins the next step of the
argument by dividing all human operations and their
goals into two classes.

> But a certain difference is found among
> ends; some are activities, others are
> products apart from the activities that
> produce them. Where there are ends apart
> from the actions, it is the nature of the
> product to be better than the activities.[48]

St. Thomas comments on the two types of human
operations.[49] The first type--operations like seeing,
willing and thinking--are a direct actualization of the
capacities which are inherent in man. The result of
these operations is not to perfect some outside thing
but to complete the nature of man himself. Consequently
these operations are chosen for their own sake; they
are goals in themselves.

The second type--operations like sawing or healing--
have results which pass over into some external work
like a house or a patient. These operations are not
sought for their own sake but for the sake of the work
or product. These operations are not goals in themselves but are merely means to the goal. Consequently
they are less important than the goals.

Works or products are less important than operations
which are goals in themselves. While the former are
only instruments used by man for his perfection, the
latter constitute the very perfection of man himself.

Having shown that there are two orders of human
operations, Aristotle proceeds to show how there is
a highest goal in the order of production and then in
the order of immanent operations. A summary of these
arguments will suffice for our purposes.

Experience in the realm of the productive arts
shows that there are many operations and goals.
Experience also shows that the goals of some arts are

---

cadit supra malum" Sent. Ethic., I,1,160-164.

[48]E.N. I,1,1094a3-6.

[49]Sent. Ethic., I,1,192-210.

subordinate to those of higher arts; e.g., the arts of bridle making and of riding are subordinate to the military art. Thus the higher goal of the higher art is the reason why lesser goals are pursued. Since order exists among the arts, there must be a cause; namely, the pursuit of some highest goal by some highest architectonic or master art.

Experience in the realm of immanent operations shows that there are many such goals or goods. For example, operations like seeing, thinking and willing, being sought for their own sake, are goods for their own sake. Now these goods must be either final or intermediate. If they are neither, they are not goods. Now if there is a final good among them, the case is proven. But if one denies the existence of a final good, then all goods must be intermediate; i.e., one good must be chosen for the sake of another ad infinitum. If however all goods are intermediate, they are not goods at all because they lack a cause. For the intermediate goods of any order are caused by the pursuit of the highest good of that order. Yet the facts show at the very least that intermediate goods exist. Therefore, there must be some highest good or operation which is pursued for its own sake, all other goods being pursued for its sake.

The statement that some highest human good exsists calls for some clarification. One may understand the statement to mean that, whatever man does, he does it for the sake of what he takes to be his highest aim in life. So understood, this statement tells how men actually operate. Yet experience shows that this good may be either real or only apparent. The reason is that, while all men have by their very nature the possibility of eventually performing an operation which completes his nature, not all men choose to realize this possibility or capacity. The result is the pursuit of both real and apparent goals.

The conclusion of the introductory argument then is that there exists some operation which constitutes man's proper and final good. It should be pursued for its own sake, all other goods being pursued for its sake.

One should note that the basic foundation of the introductory argument is the claim that many human goals or goods do indeed exist. This claim already involves the necessities which the analysis simply spells out.

If, however, one does not grant the validity of the initial experience of the fact, he will not accept its metaphysical and epistemological account. For example, if one holds that man's ability to know the facts must be first justified by a critical method which takes as its starting point something other than man's initial experience of the facts, he will consider the introductory argument uncritical or naive. Again, if one holds that there is a radical distinction between "fact" and "value",[50] he will not accept that man's choice of goods is as much a fact as the movement of plants and animals towards their goals are facts.

The above observations are made, not to initiate a defense of Aristotle's and Thomas' starting points, but to illustrate how crucial these starting points are.

So far what has Thomas accomplished? He has distinguished man's proper good from that of the whole universe and of non-rational agents. In so doing, he has provided the material, not just for a practical, but also for a speculative inquiry into the nature of this good. If one seeks to know man's proper good simply for the sake of truth, one then has the object of a speculative science, specifically the science of man or, more generally, the science of metaphysics. What shape would this inquiry take? The introductory argument has shown that man's highest good is a final goal and must be an operation of some kind. Consequently, the inquirer must first analyze all human operations to see which of them fulfills the condition of a final cause; namely, what is sought for its own sake, all else being sought for its sake. When the inquirer sees that this operation is the activity of contemplation, he has attained the goal of his quest.

If, however, one wishes to treat the material of man's proper good for the sake of acquiring that good, he has the object of a practical inquiry. As the

---

[50]For a discussion of this distinction from the viewpoint of traditional metaphysics, see the article by Joseph Owens, "Value and Metaphysics" in The Future of Metaphysics, ed. Robert E. Wood (Chicago: Quadrangle Press, 1970), pp. 204-208.

following will show, this is the type of inquiry that
Aristotle seeks to initiate. He asks: "Will not the
knowledge of it, then, have a great influence on life?"[51]
Thomas comments "that from the fact that there is some
highest goal of human actions, the knowledge of it is
a great addition to life; that is, it will be a great
help to the whole of human life."[52] The knowledge of
man's proper good, then, is to be sought, not as an end
in itself, but as an aid or instrument to be used in
the actual attainment of the goal.

How necessary to man is this practical scientific
knowledge? Aristotle goes on to remark: "Shall we not
like archers who have a mark to aim at be more likely
to hit upon what is right?"[53] St. Thomas comments:

> This is evident for the following reason:
> nothing which is directed to another can be
> acquired by man unless he knows that to
> which it is directed. This is evident from
> the example of the archer who shoots the
> arrow straight by aiming at the target to
> which he directs it.[54]

Though the text seems clear enough, there is a
question here. Does Thomas mean to say that, just as
the archer cannot direct his arrow unless he first sees
the target, so man cannot direct his life unless he
first knows the precise nature of his proper goal? If
Thomas means this, he is saying that the student of
practical science cannot be a good man unless he has
already completed the demonstration concerning the

---

[51]E.N. I,2,1094a22.

[52]"Concludit . . . ex quo est aliquis optimus finis
rerum humanorum, cognitio eius habet magnum incrementum
ad vitam, id est multum auxilium confert ad totam vitam
humanam" Sent. Ethic., I,2,58-61.

[53]E.N. I,2,1094a23.

[54]"Quod quidem apparet tali ratione: nihil quod in
alterum dirigitur potest homo recte assequi nisi cognos-
cat illud ad quod dirigendum est, et hoc apparet per
exemplum sagittatoris qui directe emittit sagittam at-
tendens ad signum ad quod eam dirigit. . ." Sent. Ethic.,
I,2,61-67.

nature of his proper good. On this view of the matter, the student would somehow have to live by moral norms accepted provisionally until he could confirm them by scientific demonstration. He would have to live by mere opinion until he gained true knowledge. The knowledge of moral science, then, would be essential to the leading of a good life.

Yet Aristotle, and St. Thomas commenting upon his statement, say only that moral science is a great _help_ to human life. Why just a great help? The answer is that both know from experience that there are good men who do not know moral philosophy. Thus in their view the knowledge absolutely essential for leading a good life is that of the prudent man. Through his habituation the judgment of the good man has certitude, not merely opinion, about what is good in the particular.[55] Now the student of moral science must already be a man of this type. For only in the hands of such a man will scientific knowledge be a useful instrument.[56]

Thus the analogy which Thomas makes between the archer and the agent should be interpreted as follows. Just as the archer cannot direct his arrow unless he sees the target, so the agent cannot direct his life _scientifically_ unless he first knows the precise nature of man's proper good. Upon this precise knowledge of the goal rests the knowledge of the universal norms appropriate to it. Demonstrated knowledge of the goal is essential to the knowledge of moral science but not to knowledge of prudence.

---

[55] See below, pp. 126-127.

[56] If the student is already a good man, one may wonder why he should bother to study moral science. To answer that question one should recall that for Aristotle moral science is the same as political science. Now "laws are the 'works' of the political art" (_E.N._ X,9,1181a1). Hence the aim of the study is to prepare the student to be a law maker. In this endeavor there is no substitute for experience. Nevertheless, intellectual reflection upon experience can be of help in practical matters. For the study emphasizes what is common to all men before descending to the varying particulars of action. Knowing what is common is a help when reflecting upon a community.

What is the nature of this precise knowledge of
the goal? Is the mark or target that the good man aims
at simply the speculative knowledge that the activity
of contemplation is man's highest goal? No. For a man
may know this truth without necessarily choosing to
live by it. Or he may somehow desire this goal without
having the real will or ability to attain it. The mark
that the good man aims at is set by a man's virtue, which
is defined as the state of character by which the agent
steers between excess and defect in order to attain the
mean.[57] The good man embodies this mean as an operating
principle of action. Now when this mark is articulated
in the universals of practical science, the result is
far more than a merely speculative knowledge of man's
nature and goal. It is the articulation of an actual
working principle.

There is, then, a great difference between the
speculative and practical consideration of man's proper
good. Yet one can take the edge off this difference
by reading the introductory argument as follows. Aristotle expends so much effort in demonstrating metaphy-
sically that some highest good exists because without
such a demonstration the moral philosopher has nothing
to inquire into. In other words, Aristotle is laying
down the foundations or first principles of moral
philosophy.

To argue in the above manner, however, is to forget
that the first principles of moral science are to be
found in the prudential knowledge of the good man himself, not in the speculative study of man's nature. The
good man already knows in an experiential way what his
goal is and how to attain it.

But if the good man already knows experientially
what his proper goal is, why does Aristotle bother to
write his long introduction? The answer, as was already
noted in the case of St. Thomas[58] is that the purpose
of the introduction is to define the object of moral
science. This process is certainly of use to the good

---

[57]For a discussion of virtue as the mean, see
below, p. 98, note 15.
[58]See above, pp. 50-51.

man because it aids him not only in reflecting upon his
own experience but in attaining a clear intellectual
grasp of his own object compared to those of the other
sciences. Insofar as moral philosophy, unlike prudence,
is a purely intellectual virtue, the practical thinker
can certainly benefit from the aid supplied by the metaphysician. Yet the power of the argument comes, not
primarily from the rigorous detail of the demonstration,
but from the force supplied by experience of the good
man.

The procedure of Aristotle illustrates this point;
namely, how the moral philosopher, while using the
knowledge of the speculative thinker, argues primarily
from his own first principles in his own way. In chapter
four, the beginning of the Ethics proper, Aristotle
answers the question of what man's highest good is in
the following way:

> Verbally there is very general agreement;
> for both the general run of men and people
> of superior refinement say that it is hap-
> piness, and identify living well and doing
> well with being happy . . . .[59]

By a single stroke of induction from ordinary
experience, Aristotle concludes that there is such a
thing as happiness. No demonstration is used here
though, as we have seen, there are many steps indeed
between the fact that there are many human goods to
the conclusion that there must be some highest human
good. In the text above, he goes on to note that,
while the many think that happiness consists in the
pursuit of pleasure or riches, the few say that it is
the pursuit of honor or virtue. And how does Aristotle
decide which of these goods is man's true good? He
notes that pleasures and riches are goals fit only for
beasts. The practice of virtue turns out to be man's
highest good. Clearly the force behind this rather
sketchy argument is the experience of the good man
himself. In the light of this experience Aristotle
does not expend much effort in refuting the views of
the many. And yet, as even a brief glance at the De
Anima will show, Aristotle expends a great deal of
effort in pointing our the difference between the
powers of animals and of man. But does the good man

---

[59]E.N. I,4,1095a16-19.

learning practical science need such elaborate arguments to see the difference between what is appropriate to man and to animals?

In chapter seven of Book One, however, Aristotle shows how experiential knowledge may be refined into a formal definition of happiness. Even a cursory reading of this section shows that the argument is but an extension and elaboration of the introductory argument. Speculative knowledge, then, is certainly used as an aid. But it is an aid tailored to the needs of practical argument.

St. Thomas takes no exception to Aristotle in commenting on these sections. To illustrate just how closely Thomas agrees with Aristotle, we will record a passage from Aristotle and the corresponding comments of Thomas.

> For a carpenter and a geometer investigate the right angle in different ways; the former does so insofar as the right angle is useful for his work, while the latter inquires what it is or what sort of thing it is; for he is a spectator of the truth. We must act in the same way, then, in all other matters as well, that our main task may not be subordinated to minor questions.[60]

St. Thomas comments:

> He says that the carpenter, who is a practical man, and a geometrician, who is a speculative thinker, study a straight line in different ways. A practical man, a carpenter, studies the line insofar as it is useful to his work as, for example, in cutting wood or in doing something of that type. But the geometrician studies the nature and quality of a line by considering its properties and potentialities because he aims only at the truth. Accordingly, one must proceed in the first way in the other practical sciences to avoid the mistake of having more discussion in a practical

---

[60]_E.N._ I,7,1098a29-33.

science about things that do not belong
to its goal than do belong. An example
is if in moral science someone wishes to
treat of all the things pertaining to the
intellect and to the other parts of the soul
so that he says more about them than about
human operations themselves. It is a serious
defect in any science for a man to involve
himself too much in questions outside his
science.[61]

Just as the line, a non-operable, may be considered
in practical science, so may the nature of man, also a
non-operable, be considered in moral science. By the
same token speculative truth may be utilized by the
moral philosopher in his own way for his own purpose.
This use of the truth about the non-operable, however,
does not make it the material object of practical
science. For, as we have seen earlier,[62] the material
object is simply human operations because, being the
products of choice, they alone essentially involve
choice. Certainly the nature of reality itself is a
factor which influences choice. But particular choices

---

[61]"Unde dicit quod tector, id est artifex operativus,
et geometra, qui est speculativus, differenter inquirunt
de linea recta. Artifex quidem operativus, ut pote car-
pentarius, inquirit de linea recta quantum est utile
ad opus, utpote ad secundum ligna vel aliquid alius
huiusmodi faciendum; sed geometra inquirit quid est
linea recta et quale quid est, considerando proprietates
et passiones ipsius, quia geometra intendit solam
speculationem veritatis. Et secundum hunc modum faciendum est in aliis scientiis operativis, ut non sequatur
hoc inconveniens ut in scientia operativa fiant plures
sermones ad opera non pertinentes illis sermonibus qui
sunt circa opera, puta, si in hac scientia morali aliquis
vellet pertractare omnia quae pertinent ad rationem et
alias partes animae, oporteret plura de hoc dicere quam
de ipsis operibus. Est enim in unaquaque scientia vitiosum ut homo multum immoretur in his quae sunt extra
scientiam" Sent. Ethic., I,11,77-95. Another text showing how speculative truths are to be used in practical
science is: E.N. I,13,1102a17-26; St. Thomas, I,19,58-85

[62]See above, p. 9.

are determined by man himself and so are the objects of a science which take into account this variable goal.

In conclusion, this chapter has shown first, that while the metaphysician defines the object of moral philosophy, he does not supply the foundations or first principles of that science. Second, while human operations may be considered speculatively, they constitute the object of moral philosophy only when considered practically. Third, the moral philosopher uses the truths of speculative science in his own way for his own purposes.

CHAPTER IV

THE RELATIONSHIP OF MORAL PHILOSOPHY
TO THE ARTS AND TO METAPHYSICS

Following the order of Aristotle's presentation, this chapter will discuss the nature of moral science. At this point it is obvious that this science is practical. But what is not yet clear is the precise relationship of this practical science to the productive arts and to metaphysics.

Aristotle, having determined that the object of ethics is the knowledge of man's highest good sought for the sake of action, begins his treatment by declaring that "we must try, in outline at least, to determine what it is, and of which of the sciences or capacities it is the object."[1]

Aristotle answers that the study of realizing man's highest good "would seem to belong to the most authoritative art and that which is most truly the master art. And politics appears to be of this nature. . . ."[2] To prove this point Aristotle proceeds in his usual manner; i.e., he first reviews the facts of experience before trying to explain them in terms of their cause. In this case the facts are determined by the manner in which the civic community in the Greek culture operates or makes choices about its common concerns either by the formal process of making laws of by the informal process o following customary practices. The investigation of these facts shows that the basic concerns of the community

> ordain which of the sciences should be studied in a state, and which each class of citizen should learn and up to what point they should learn them; and we see even the most highly esteemed of capacities to fall under this, e.g. strategy, economics, rhetoric. . . .[3]

---

[1] E.N. I,2,1094a26-27.

[2] E.N. I,2,1094a28-29.

[3] E.N. I,2,1094b1-4.

Here Aristotle is noting as a matter of fact that
the interest of the community regulates all the human
operations--both speculative and practical--of the individuals within that community. What is the cause or
explanation of this fact? Aristotle answers that, since
politics "legislates as to what we are to do and what we
are to abstain from, the end of this science must include
those of the others, so that this end must be the good
of man."[4] The explanation of the fact, then, is that
the goal of politics is the highest good of man. Since
this goal includes that of all the activities of art
and science, politics commands the operations of all
the sciences.

In calling the science which treats of man's highest good politics, Aristotle is articulating the ancient
Greek conviction that man attains his full perfection
only as a participant in the civic community. The goal
of happiness in an afterlife is not a very important
consideration.[5] Consequently, the pursuit of happiness
in the context of the civic community regulates the
actions of the family and of the individual. Since the
Politics completes and makes more specific the treatment
of man's good as broadly outlined in the Ethics, politics
and moral philosophy are the same for Aristotle.[6]

What is the reaction of St. Thomas to this Greek
conception of moral science? St. Thomas simply comments
on the text as it stands. It must be remembered, however, that he has already made his position clear in
his own introduction. There, after defining moral
philosophy in general as the study of human action as
directed to a goal, he proceeds to divide this study
into three parts: "the first considers the operations
of an individual man directed to a goal and is called

---

[4]E.N. I,2,1094b5-7.

[5]Aristotle says: " . . . is it also the case that
a man is happy when he is dead? Or is not this quite
absurd, especially of us who say that happiness is an
activity?" E.N. I,10,1100a13-14.

[6]For a differing opinion see R.A. Gauthier, and
J.Y. Jolif, L'Ethique a Nicomaque (Louvain and Paris
1958-1959), II,2.

<u>monostica</u>."[7] The second and third parts are domestic
economy and politics.

        This division of St. Thomas, as Joseph Owens points
out,[8] has its origin in Christian tradition, where perfect
happiness is an operation of the individual in the next
life. Consequently this tradition does not equate moral
philosophy with politics, which treats only of man's
good in this life. Within this Christian framework,
however, St. Thomas can still accommodate the more
limited view of Aristotle. For St. Thomas also considers
man to be a "social animal" (I,1,55) who, therefore,
needs the family and the community to attain his perfection. This perfection is imperfect or limited.[9]

        The superimposing of a Christian framework over the
original Greek structure is quite in order if one accepts the premise that the first principles of moral
science must be drawn from the experience of the prudent man. Now the prudent man exemplifies the best of
his culture. Therefore it is quite natural to expect
the moral science of an ancient Greek and of a medieval
theologian to differ in important respects. Clearly
the basic principle which Aristotle and St. Thomas
hold in common also accounts for the areas in which
they differ.

        Returning to the original point, we note that
Aristotle considers politics to be an archetectonic or

------

[7]" . . . moralis philosophia in tres partes dividi-
tur, quorum prima considerat operationes unius hominis
ordinatas ad finem quae vocatur monostica. . ." <u>Sent.
Ethic.</u>, I,1,100-102.

    [8]Joseph Owens, "Aquinas as Aristotelian Commenta-
tor," <u>Commemorative</u> <u>Studies</u>: <u>St.</u> <u>Thomas</u> <u>Aquinas</u> <u>1274-
1974</u>, pp. 229-230, note 41.

    [9]Every so often St. Thomas will point out that
Aristotle is speaking only of happiness in this life.
See I,9,162-163; I,15,52-56; I,17,146-147. The point
is brought out most clearly in the commentary on the
<u>Sentences</u>. "Contemplatio autem Dei est duplex. Una per
creaturas, quae imperfecta est, ratione jam dicta, in
qua contemplatione Philosophus, X <u>Ethic</u>., . . . felici-
tatem contemplativam posuit, quae tamen est felicitas
vitae; et ad hanc ordinatur tota cognitio philosophica,
quae ex rationibus creaturarum procedit." <u>In</u> <u>I</u> <u>Sent.</u>,

master science. In the _Metaphysics_, however, he
considers metaphysics to be the master science. "And
the science which knows to what end each thing must be
done is the most authoritative of the sciences; and
this end is the good of that thing, and in general the
supreme good in the whole of nature."[10] Furthermore,
it has already been shown[11] that the art which produces
the best and most important product is a master art.
Obviously all of these studies cannot be a master
science in the same respect. In what respect is each
a master science?

To deal with this question, St. Thomas develops the
distinction implicit in the Aristotelian text between
the exercise and the specification of any operation.
By means of this distinction, he considers the relationship of politics to the productive arts and then to the
speculative sciences:

> For political science dictates to practical
> science in regard to the exercise of its
> act (that is, whether it should act or not)
> and in regard to the specification of its
> act. For it dictates to the smith not only
> whether he will exercise his act but even
> that it be exercised in a certain way as,
> for example, to make a knife. Both of these
> aspects of operations are able to be ordered
> to the end of human life.[12]

Politics dictates both the exercise and the specification of the operations of the productive arts.
Concerning their exercise, politics determines whether
the craftsman will operate or not. For the craftsman

Prol., q.1,a.1, Solut.; ed. Mandonnet, (Paris: 1929),
I, pp. 7-8.

[10]_Metaphysics_ I,2,982b4-5.

[11]See above, p. 73.

[12]"Nam practicae scientiae praecipit politica et
quantum ad usum eius, ut scilicet operetur vel non operetur, et quantum ad determinationem actus: praecipit
enim fabro non solum quod utatur sua arte, sed etiam
quod sic utatur, tales cultellos faciens; utrumque
enim est ordinatum ad finem humanae vitae." _Sent. Ethic._,
I,2,128-134.

as such has only the capacity to produce. But the actualization of this capacity depends upon the power of the craftsman to choose. If his choice is good, then it will be in line with the judgment that this choice furthers man's highest good. Since the goal of politics is to determine what should be chosen for the sake of man's highest good, it will ultimately be the ruler who dictates the exercise of the operations of the productive arts.

Concerning the specification of productive operations, political science also lays down the rule. Since the ruler determines whether it is tools of war or of peace that are needed by the community, he supplies the reason why the craftsman makes swords or plows. The kind of work that the workman performs is determined ultimately by the ruler.

The basic reason why even the most architectonic of the productive arts is subordinate to politics is that both the exercise and the specification of productive operations "are able to be ordered to the end of human life." Productive operations, and indeed all human operations, can be ordered to man's good because man only chooses to operate when he sees his act as furthering his highest good. Since the products are by nature instruments, they can be ordered to suit man's own purposes.

Next St. Thomas considers the relationship between politics and the speculative sciences:

> Political science dictates to speculative science only in regard to the exercise and not in regard to the specification of the operation. For political science orders that some teach or learn geometry. Insofar as acts of this kind are voluntary, they pertain to moral matter and are able to be ordered to the end of human life. Political science, however, does not dictate to the geometer what he should conclude about the triangle, for the conclusion is neither subject to the human will nor can it be ordered to the end of human life but depends on the very nature of things.[13]

---

[13]"Sed scientiae speculativae praecipit civilis solum quantum ad usum, non autem quantum ad determination

But the political philosopher does not dictate the specification of any speculative operation. For speculative operations are entities caused by man for the sake of cognitionally becoming one with reality. Their object is the truth about the way things are. Thus it is the nature of reality itself that specifies these operations. And so the ruler has no control about what the metaphysician says or concludes concerning the nature of things. For any conclusion about the nature of things "is neither subject to the human will nor can it be ordered to the end of human life but depends on the very nature of things."

On the basis, then, that it is the nature of reality itself that specifies speculative operations, politics has no power over speculative science. For politics is master only of those arts and sciences whose end is either some product or the attainment of man's perfection.

At this point, what can one conclude about the relationship of metaphysics to moral philosophy? Speculatively speaking, metaphysics is the master science. Why? Because, as St. Thomas says, "it considers the ultimate end of the whole universe and is the most important science of all."[14] Why should the consideration of the truth about the ultimate end make metaphysics the master science? Aristotle answers that "wisdom must be scientific knowledge of the highest objects. . . Of the highest objects, we say: for it would be strange to think that the art of politics, or practical wisdom, is the best knowledge, since man is not the best thing in the world."[15] Because metaphysics

operis; ordinat enim politica quod aliqui doceant vel addiscant geometriam, huiusmodi enim actus in quantum sunt voluntarii pertinent ad materiam moralem et sunt ordinabiles ad finem humanae vitae; non autem praecipit politicus geometrae quid de triangulo concludat, hoc enim non subiacet humanae voluntati nec est ordinabile humanae vitae, sed dependet ex ipsa rerum ratione." Sent. Ethic., I,2,134-144.

[14]"Nam ultimum finem totius universi considerat scientia divina, quae est in respectu omnium principalissima. Sent. Ethic., I,2,197-198.

[15]E.N. VI,7,1141a19-21.

deals with realities which are more perfect than man, its consideration of these realities is more perfect than any speculative or practical consideration dealing with man himself. Consequently, the exercise of this science constitutes man's highest activity or perfection. For through the act of knowledge he becomes one in a way with the most perfect things.

Yet while reality itself specifies the intellectual activity of the metaphysician, the exercise of his activity is determined according as it promotes man's perfection in a particular time and place. Thus the exercise of the activity is determined, not by the metaphysician as metaphysician, but by the man as moral agent. At certain times, for example, a man's perfection may require that he take up the sword rather than teach or contemplate. In the realm of the exercise of action, then, the moral philosopher, not the metaphysician, is supreme.

CHAPTER V

THE METHOD OF MORAL PHILOSOPHY

Chapter three showed in a preliminary way that,
while the object of speculative science is necessary or
unchanging, the object of moral science is contingent
or variable.[1] It also projected essential differences
between the two kinds of science that follow from the
differences in object. This chapter, following the
order of Aristotle's text and the commentary of St.
Thomas, will supply the textual basis for those earlier
projections.

The first section will show that, while the necessary object of speculative science requires that
universal statements of truth be unchanging, the contingent object of moral science requires that universal
standards of action be variable. The second section
will draw out the further consequence that the method
of moral science is synthetic while that of speculative
science is analytic. The third section will draw out
the final consequence that, while prudence is not an
essential factor in speculative reasoning, it is essential to practical reasoning.

I. The Difference Between Speculative and Practical
    Universals

The basic argument of this section deals with the
following questions. While there is no particular
difficulty about the notion that the necessary object
of speculative reason is treated in universal terms,
how can the variable object of practical reason be so
treated? If this object can be treated universally,
must there be a basic difference between the practical
and speculative universal? Furthermore, would this
difference indicate that there is also a basic difference between practical and speculative truth, the
standard of the former being right desire while that
of the latter being the way reality is? But if the
standards of practical and speculative reason do differ,
is the former as objective as the latter? Finally, can

_____

[1]See above, p. 57.

89

these standards be located in objective reality or must the standard of practical reason be located in another manner?

Concerning the first question, Aristotle begins the chapter[2] by describing the subject matter or object of moral science.[3] St. Thomas comments as follows:

> The subject matter of morals is of such a nature that finished certitude is not suitable to it. And this is clear from the two kinds of things which seem to belong to the subject matter of morals. First and foremost, virtuous works, which here he calls just deeds, belong to the subject matter of morals. Political science treats mainly of these matters about which there is no agreed opinion among men. Rather there are great differences in the way that men judge these matters, and manifold error occurs. For certain things which are thought to be just and noble by some are held to be unjust and ignoble by others according to differences in times, places and persons. What is thought to be evil at one time or in one region is not considered as evil at another time or in another region. . . .[4]

---

[2]E.N. I,3,1094b 11-19.

[3]The term "materia" is here translated as subject or subject matter. These latter are equivalent to objec

[4]"Materia autem moralis talis est quod non est ei conveniens perfecta certitudo. Et hoc manifestat per duo genera rerum quae videntur ad materiam moralem pertinere. Primo namque et principaliter ad materiam moralem pertinent opera virtuosa, quae vocat hic justa, de quibus principaliter intendit civilis scientia, circa quae non habetur certa sententia hominum, sed magna differentia est in hoc quod homines de his iudicant; et in hoc multiplex error contingit, nam quaedam sunt quae a quibusdam reputantur iusta et honesta, a quibusdam autem iniusta et inhonesta, secundum differentiam temporum et locorum et personarum; aliquid enim reputatur vitiosum uno tempore aut in una regione quod in alio tempore aut in alia regione non reputatur vitiosum. . ." Sent. Ethic. I,3,17-32.

A little later St. Thomas, continuing his comments upon the text of Aristotle, goes on to show that the same variety of opinion exists about external goods. He concludes: "Thus it is evident that the subject matter of moral science is variable and without formal exactitude, not allowing of complete certitude."[5]

In maintaining that the subject matter of morals is variable and, therefore, does not allow of finished certitude, St. Thomas implicitly contrasts moral with speculative science, whose subject matter is necessary and, therefore, allows of finished certitude. Upon what evidence does he base this contrast? It is that the subject matter is about virtuous works. As a sign of the variability of this matter, Thomas notes the fact that there is no agreed opinion among men about it. But why should this fact be a sign that the subject matter itself is variable? Surely there are also great differences of opinion among men about speculative matters. But here one does not conclude that the subject matter is variable but only that many men are wrong in their opinions. Why not draw the same conclusion about the subject matter of morals?

The answer is that good actions themselves vary. For example, in one region a certain punishment may be just while in another region that same punishment may be unjust. Again, for one person it may be wrong to fast but for another it may be right. Again, at one time a person should retreat from battle but at another time he should stand. Thus the goodness of the same physical act varies with the circumstances of person, time and place. Consequently, besides illegitimate there are also legitimate variations in the judgments of men about the justice or injustice of human actions.

The next question is: how can the variable or changing subject matter of moral science be treated scientifically, i.e., be articulated in universal terms? Some maintain that the variable subject matter precludes such articulation. St. Thomas, continuing to comment upon the text of Aristotle (I,3,1094b16), notes: "Owing to such differences /of opinion in moral matters/ some

─────────────
[5]"Et sic manifestum est quod materia moralis est varia et deformis, non habens omnimodum certitudinem" Sent. Ethic., I,3,45-47.

91

maintain that nothing at all is just or noble by nature but only by law. About this opinion more will be said in Book V of this work."[6]

For some thinkers the variations in men's opinions are a sign that human actions are not essentially or by nature just or unjust. For them human actions are initially indifferent and are made just or unjust by the law of the community. Consequently, there can be no universal norms which apply to all men irrespective of the law of the community. Moral science, then, is not possible.

St. Thomas, however, implies that certain actions are just or noble by nature. Consequently, such actions may be articulated in universal norms which apply to all men. According to Thomas, then, moral science is possible.

For further discussion of the matter, St. Thomas refers the reader to Book Five of the Ethics. There Aristotle, having given several examples of legal justice, which varies from community to community, says: "Now some think that all justice is of this sort, because that which is by nature is unchangeable and has everywhere the same force (a fire burns both here and in Persia), while they see change in things recognized as just."[7]

Aristotle's opponents argue that if there are naturally just actions, their nature should be as unchanging as the nature of fire, which has the same power both in Greece and in Persia. They note, however, that the notion of justice varies from community to community. Consequently, they conclude that all matters of justice are changeable and, therefore, cannot be articulated in universal norms which, of course, have the same power over all men independently of where they happen to live. In brief, Aristotle's opponents assume that, if there is such a thing as moral science, its object should be as necessary or unchanging as the object of speculative science. Since the object is not

---

[6] " . . . et ex ista differentia contingit quosdam opinari quod nihil esset naturaliter iustum vel honestum, sed solum secundum legispositionem; de qua quidem opinione ipse plenius aget in V huius" Sent. Ethic., I,3,33-3

[7] E.N. V,7,1134b24-26.

unchanging, it cannot be treated scientifically.

Aristotle answers that, while there may be in the case of the gods an unchanging norm of justice, "with us there is something just by nature, yet all of it is changeable; but still some is by nature, and some not by nature."[8] In effect, Aristotle answers that moral science is not required to meet the standards of speculative science. He classifies the whole subject matter, both natural and legal justice, as changeable. St. Thomas, reaffirming this position, comments: ". . . although all things which are just for us change in some way, nevertheless certain things are naturally just."[9]

So far the terms "changeable" or "variable" and the terms "unchanging" or "necessary" have been used to contrast the object of moral with that of speculative science. The reader should note that this is the first context in which these terms are used. But there is another context, as we shall soon see.

Now the question is: can the subject matter of morals, though variable, be articulated in universal terms? St. Thomas, commenting upon the text of Aristotle, answers:

> Those things which are natural for us are
> in the same way for the most part but are
> deficient in a few instances. For example,
> it is natural that the right hand is stronger
> than the left. This in most cases is true.
> Yet it does happen in some few cases that
> there are ambidextrous people whose left
> hand is as strong as their right. It is the
> same with naturally just things. For example,
> that a loan be repaid should be observed in
> most cases but it changes in a few instances.[10]

---

[8] E.N. V,7,1134b27-29.

[9] " . . . licet omnia quae sunt apud nos iusta aliqualiter moveantur, nihilominus quaedam sunt naturaliter iusta" Sent. Ethic., V,12,166-168.

[10] " . . . ea enim quae sunt naturalia apud nos, sunt quidem eodem modo ut in pluribus, sed ut in paucioribus deficiunt, sicut naturale est quod pars dextera sit vigoriosior quam sinistra et hoc in pluribus habet veritatem, et tamen contingit ut in paucioribus aliquos fieri

Experience shows that natural things like man have certain characteristics which usually follow upon their essential nature. Men are generally right-handed or two-eyed or biped. Consequently, the truth about these characteristics can be articulated in universal propositions which are unchanging for the most part. This view is the common teaching of Aristotle and St. Thomas, who hold that the universals of speculative science may be unchanging either always or for the most part.[11]

In the realm of action the case is similar. Experience shows that certain actions like repaying a loan are usually just. Thus they can be articulated in a universal norm which changes (_mutatur_) only in a few instances.

In the above argument the universals of both speculative and moral science are described as either changeable in a few instances or as unchangeable for the most part. This is the second context in which the terms "changeable" and "unchangeable" are used. Immediately the question arises of how the object of moral science can be called changeable while, like the object of speculative science, it allows of universals which are unchanging for the most part.

This question becomes even more acute in the following argument. Here Thomas proceeds to show that not all norms of natural justice change in a few instances; some do not change at all.

> It should be noted that, because the nature
> of even changeable things is unchanging, if

---

ambidextros qui sinistram manum habent ita valentem ut dexteram; ita enim et ea quae sunt naturaliter iusta, utputa depositum esse redendum, ut in pluribus est observandum, sed ut in paucioribus mutatur" _Sent_. _Ethic_., V,12,187-196.

[11]Aristotle says: " . . . all reasoning proceeds from necessary or general premises, the conclusion being necessary if the premises are necessary and general if the premises are general" (_AP_ I,30,87b21-25). St. Thomas comments: "Omnis syllogismus demonstrativus aut procedit ex propositionibus necessariis, aut ex propositionibus quae sunt verae ut frequenter." _In Posteriorum Analyticorum_, Spiazzi (Turin: Marietti, 1964) Bk.I, lect.43, no.373, p.304.

what is natural in us belongs to the nature
of man himself, it changes in no way. For
example, man is an animal. Those things
which follow upon nature--dispositions,
action and motion--are changeable in a few
instances. Similarly, those things which
belong to the nature of justice itself in
no way can be changed. For example, one
should not steal, since stealing is to do
an unjust thing. But things which follow
upon the nature of justice change in a few
instances.[12]

Because the essential nature of man remains the
same throughout the process of change, it may be articulated in a universal definition whose truth does not
change at all. Now in the sphere of action, certain
deeds are essentially or by nature just while others
are essentially unjust. Consequently, these deeds may
be articulated in universal norms whose correctness
does not change at all.[13] This teaching is in accord
with Aristotle who, in Book II of the Ethics, says that
murder, theft and adultery are always wrong and "it is
not possible to be right in regard to them."

---

[12]"Est tamen attendendum quod, quia rationes etiam
mutabilium sunt immutabiles, si quid est nobis naturale
quasi pertinens ad ipsam hominis rationem nullo modo
mutatur, puta hominem esse animal, quae autem consequuntur naturam, puta dispositiones, actiones et motus,
mutantur ut in paucioribus; et similiter etiam illa,
quae pertinent ad ipsam iustitiae rationem nullo modo
possunt mutari, puta non esse furandum, quod est iniustum
facere, illa vero quae consequuntur mutantur ut in
minori parte" Sent. Ethic., V,12,197-207.

[13]In the Summa Thomas shows the same concern in showing that there are certain norms of justice which are
immutable. Objection Two states: "But it is stated in
the same book (Ethic. V) that nothing is so universally
just as not to be subject to change in regard to some
men." S.T. I-II, 94, 4. St. Thomas answers: "The saying of the Philosopher is to be understood of things
that are naturally just, not as general principles, but
as conclusions drawn from them, having rectitude in the
majority of cases, but failing in a few." S.T. I-II, 94,
4, ad 2.

Thomas then proceeds to discuss matters of legal justice. Commenting upon Aristotle, he says

> that legally just things are absolutely changeable. . . . Things which are not naturally just but are made so by man are not the same everywhere. For example, the same punishment for theft is not imposed everywhere.[14]

There are certain actions which, when described in the abstract, are neither just nor unjust. Their nature is entirely variable as far as justice is concerned. They can be made just, however, by means of the law. But considered in themselves, these acts are too variable to allow of being articulated in norms which hold for all or nearly all men.

The answer to the question of how the variable subject matter of moral science can be articulated in universal norms is clear enough. There are norms of natural justice which are unchangeable either always or for the most part. Thus moral science is possible. Yet there is a problem about this argument because the terms "changeable" and "unchangeable" have been used in two different contexts. Unless the reader understands the difference between these contexts, the use of the same terms may lead to problems.

Some of these problems are as follows. If there are norms of natural justice which are immutable, why cannot one have the same certitude about their correctness as he has about the necessary truths of speculative science? If he can have a finished certitude about the truth that man is a rational animal, why cannot he have the same certitude about the norm that murder is always wrong? Yet St. Thomas explicitly states that the variable nature of the object of morals does not allow of the certitude characteristic of speculative science. But why not?

Again, it would seem that if the subject matter of morals is really variable or changeable, it cannot be

---

[14]" . . . ostendit qualiter iusta legalia sunt mutabilia indifferenter . . . iusta quae non sunt naturalia, sed per homines posita, non sunt eadem ubique, sicut non ubique eadem poena imponitur furi" Sent. Ethic., V,12,209-220.

articulated in universal norms. For matters of legal justice are entirely variable; and they cannot be articulated in universal norms which hold always or for the most part. On the other hand, if the subject matter of morals can be articulated in universal norms, the subject matter must be, like that of speculative science, unchanging either always or for the most part. If this is so, then how can Thomas contrast the changing object of moral science with the unchanging object of speculative science?

Again, it seems that one can save the scientific character of political science by restricting its treatment to matters of natural justice, thereby excluding matters of legal justice. But what is gained in intelligibility is lost in practicality. How practical can a political science be which omits considerations of legal justice?

The solution to all of these problems lies in clarifying the way moral science is similar to and distinct from speculative science. When this clarification is made, the problem about the ambiguous use of the terms "changeable" and "unchangeable" will be cleared up.

Speculative and moral science are similar in that their universals originate from the observation of particular instances, all of which have a nature or essence of some type. In speculative science the typical instances are natural substances. Now reflection upon the particular instances of man, for example, gives rise to the following types of propositions. First, the fact that man's essential nature is unchanging gives rise to the unchanging truth that man is a rational animal. Second, the fact that most men are right-handed gives rise to the universal truth that men are right-handed for the most part. And third, the fact that a man is sitting does not give rise to any universal truth at all. There is no necessary connection between the nature of man and the fact that a man is sitting.

In practical science the typical instances are human actions. Reflection upon these instances also gives rise to three types of norms. First, the fact that each act of murder is unjust gives rise to the unchanging norm that murder is unjust. Second, the fact that the repayment of loans is usually just gives rise to a norm which is unchanging for the most part.

And third, the fact that a particular punishment for theft is in itself neither just nor unjust does not give rise to any universal norms at all.

In this context the terms "unchangeable" and "changeable" are used to contrast the scientific with the non-scientific. Since all science deals with both the essential natures and consequent properties of their subjects, they employ universals which are unchanging either always or for the most part. If a subject is entirely changeable in nature, it cannot be scientifically treated.

The context changes, however, when speculative and practical are compared in view of their differing objects. Here the terms "changeable" or "variable" describe the object of moral science while the terms "necessary" or "unchanging" describe the object of speculative science. How do the objects differ? The natures of such things like men, plants and animals--all treated in speculative science--are stable or fixed. They stay the same while undergoing the process of change. But particular instances of good actions, while they have the nature of being good, have not a stable or fixed nature. For good actions have the nature of a mean, which is the right choice existing between excess and defect and which is determined in relationship to the prudent man.[15] Now this mean varies according to differences in the circumstances of person, time and place. Consequently, the universal norms articulating this mean are variable or flexible in nature, not fixed or stable.

When, therefore, the objects of speculative and moral science are being contrasted, the term "unchangeable" means stable, rigid, or fixed while the term "changeable" means variable or flexible.

The following texts bring out quite clearly this difference between the objects of moral and of

---

[15]Aristotle defines virtue, the source from which good actions come, as "a state of character concerned with choice, lying in a mean, i.e. the mean relative to us, this being determined by a rational principle, and by that principle by which the man of practical wisdom would determine it" (E.N. II,6,1107a1-3). St. Thomas explains this definition in his commentary (II,7,86-105).

speculative science. Aristotle says that "matters
concerned with conduct and questions of what is good
for us have no fixity, any more than matters of health.
The general account being of this nature, the account
of particular cases is yet more lacking in exactness.[16]

St. Thomas comments:

> the discussion of morals even in the
> universal is undetermined and variable, and
> yet it is even more undetermined if one wishes
> to descend lower by applying the discussion
> to the realm of the particular. . . .[17]

Aristotle describes, not just the particular, but
even the universal account of morals as having "no fixity" or as "lacking in exactness". Thomas comments that
the universal account is "undetermined"[18] and "variable".
Such terms cannot be used to describe the universal
account of speculative science. But they are used to
describe the account of moral science because its norms,
which always articulate a mean, include actions which
are diverse in nature. For example, the norm of courage
is undetermined or flexible enough to include such
diverse acts as retreating or advancing in battle. The
variable norm of temperance includes such acts as eating
or fasting. Even the universal prohibition against

---

[16]E.N. II,2,1104a4-7.

[17]". . . sermo moralium etiam in universalibus sit
incertus et variabilis, adhuc magis incertus est si quis
velit ulterius descendere tradendo doctrinam de singulis in speciale . . ." Sent. Ethic., II,2,71-74.

[18]The word "incertus" has been translated as undetermined in order to avoid the impression that the agent
is uncertain about the general correctness of the universal norms of moral science. The agent is not uncertain of the correctness of the norms themselves.
Rather he is uncertain of what he should do in the
particular until he has deliberated. And he must de-
liberate in some way because the norm itself is indeterminate as far as particular choices are concerned.
For example, an agent knowing that he should not murder
must know much more than this before he knows what he
should do in the particular circumstance facing him.

murder is flexible. At one time it may demand that a
murderer be punished. At another time it may demand
that one be murdered rather than murder. Because each
instance of good action is a variable mean, the universal norm articulating this mean must be flexible or
indeterminate in nature.

Aristotle summarizes the matter as follows:

> For when the thing is indefinite the rule
> also is indefinite, like the leaden rule
> used in making the Lesbian moulding; the
> rule adapts itself to the shapes of the stone
> and is not rigid, and so too the decree is
> adapted to the facts.[19]

The particular good to be done is indefinite in
two senses. First, all matters of choice as they present themselves to the agent are not yet determined
by the agent. They wait upon his deliberation and
choice before attaining their definite nature and
existence. Thus, while the object of speculative science is some definite thing to be contemplated, the object of moral science is some indefinite good to be
made definite. Second, even when the particular good
to be done has been determined by choice, that good
still has the nature of a variable mean. This mean is
indefinite because it is not wedded to a single act
like fasting or eating, advancing or retreating. Thus
the general norm articulating this mean is also indefinite or variable in nature. Consequently, practical
norms are like the leaden rule which is indeterminate
enough to be adapted to the different shapes of the
stones measured. The indeterminateness of the practical
norms is what enables them to be adapted to the variability of the deeds to be enacted.

The analogy, however, between the leaden rule and
practical norms should not be pushed too hard. After
all, the leaden rule is a definite physical reality
used to measure other already existing realities. But
practical norms articulate the habitual orientation of
the prudent man towards his proper good. Thus they are
more like a steady vision of a goal in the light of

---

[19]_E.N_. V,10,1137b30-31.

which the agent surveys his immediate circumstances to
find the means to attain that goal. But these circumstances are not the things measured. Rather the deed
to be done, the new reality to be enacted, is the thing
measured.

Another text showing the basic difference between
the stable universals of speculative science and the
flexible norms of moral science is as follows. Aristotle says:

> Now if what is healthy or good is different
> for men and for fish, but what is white or
> straight is always the same, anyone would say
> that what is wise is the same but what is
> practically wise is different . . . .[20]

St. Thomas comments:

> . . . there are certain things whose definition
> consists in a proportion or a relation to
> another. Therefore things of this type can-
> not be the same for all. It is clear that
> what is healthy and what is good is not the
> same for men and for fishes. Other things
> are predicated absolutely, as white of colored
> things and straight of figures. Because
> wisdom treats of those things which are such
> simply and in themselves (for it treats of
> first beings), everyone must say that what
> is wise is the same in all things and that
> wisdom is the same without qualification
> in regard to all. But what is prudent must
> be different in regard to different things
> because prudence is predicated according to
> proportion or relation to another.[21]

---

[20] E.N. VI,7,1141a22-25.

[21] " . . . quod quaedam sunt quorum ratio consistit
in proportione et habitudine ad aliquid et ideo huiusmodi non possunt esse eadem quantum ad omnia, sicut
patet quod non idem est sanum et bonum hominibus et
piscibus, quaedam vero dicuntur absolute, sicut album
in coloribus et rectam in figuris, et quia sapientia
est de his quae in se absolute sunt talia (est enim de
primis entium), oportet ab omnibus dici quod idem est
id quod est sapiens in omnibus et quod sit eadem sapientia simpliciter in respectu omnium; sed id quod est

The basic point to be shown is that, while the practically wise (the variable object of moral science) is different for each agent, the wise or true (the unchanging object of speculative science) is the same for each spectator. This basic point is illustrated by contrasting the nature of what is treated in moral science with that of the typical instances treated in speculative science.

Now moral science treats of good actions. But what is good is not the same for all agents because, as was shown before,[22] good includes within its definition a reference to another. A good is something needed or desired by some person or thing. For example, water is good for fish while air is good for men. Obviously the good of fish is not the same as the good for man. The instances of water and air differ essentially from one another. Yet both can be called good because they have the same proportion to those things for which they are good. In other words, the term "good" is predicated analogously of these instances.[23]

Since all goods vary with the agents seeking them, human goods vary with human agents. This truth is illustrated by the fact that a virtuous deed is defined as a mean in relation to the agent.[24] What is practically wise or prudent, then, is different for each agent. While the universal norms expressing this mean may be called the same for each agent insofar as all men should follow these norms either always or for the most part, still these norms are flexible and so require different deeds of each agent according to the variations of circumstances.

---

prudens oportet quod sit alterum apud diversos propter hoc quod prudentia dictur secundum proportionem et habitudinem ad aliquid?" Sent. Ethic., VI,6,46-59.

[22]See above, p. 69.

[23]Commenting upon Aristotle, Thomas says: "...omnia bona magis secundum analogiam, id est proportionem eandem, quantum scilicet quod visus est bonum corporis et intellectus est bonum animae" Sent. Ethic., I,7,206-211.

[24]See above, p. 98, note 15.

In the case of speculative science, its object includes both the operable and the non-operable. When these things are considered simply for the sake of truth they constitute a determinate object which is the same for all spectators. Now the typical instances treated in speculative science are non-operables such as white, right angle, man. The essential natures of these things are stable or fixed. They are defined absolutely, i.e., without any reference to another. Thus one instance is the same as another. The natures are predicated of their instances univocally. Clearly, then, the nature of these things does not change or vary for the spectator.

Yet human goods and practical norms may also be considered speculatively. When they are so considered, they become stable objects of contemplation. Their truth does not change for the spectator. For example, all spectators must agree that human goods are different for each agent, are predicated analogously and are variable in nature.

In view of the basic distinction between the unchanging object of speculative science and the variable object of moral science, the problem about certitude mentioned earlier[25] is easily solved. Because the object of speculative science is to seek for its own sake the necessary truth about things, the spectator can rest in the attainment of this truth with a finished or fully rounded certitude.

But because the object of moral science is the variable goal of action, the certitude that the practical man seeks is not primarily about the correctness of the universal norm but about the correctness of some particular deed to be done. In other words, he seeks the truth of the norm primarily for the sake of using that truth as an aid. While he has no doubt about the correctness of the norm, he nevertheless does not have a finished or fully rounded certitude about it. As undeniably correct as the norm is, that norm still opens out towards the possibilities of an infinite number of prudent choices in the particular. Since the certitude characteristic of each prudent choice is variable, so the certitude about the norm used as a guide is also

---

[25]See above, p. 96.

variable. Speculative and practical certitude, therefore
are not different because the latter is somehow held
with less conviction than the former. They are different
because the former is about the truth of universals
sought for their own sake while the latter is about the
correctness of a particular deed to be done. And as
the speculative thinker does not waver in his certitude
about the truth, so the prudent man does not waver in
his certitude about the particular good to be done.

Consequently, St. Thomas can say that the variable
object of moral science does not allow of perfect or
finished certitude and also maintain that there are
practical norms which are immutable either always or
for the most part. For the immutability of these norms
is not that of the stable or fixed universals of speculative science but of the variable norms of practical
science.

Again, the fact that practical norms are flexible
guides to action solves the problem[26] about the relationship of natural to legal justice. The norms of natural
justice are the articulations of a just ruler who has
the common good for his goal. These norms are indeterminate as far as, for example, the specific punishment
to be attached to the crime of theft. Yet the determination of such matters, though indifferent in their
general nature, is quite essential to the maintenance
of justice. Consequently, the ruler specifies[27] the
punishment in the light which the norms of justice cast
upon the particular circumstances of the community. A
legal code is the result. Another just ruler in another
community may erect a different code suitable to the
conditions of that community. Yet both codes will be
just because they are specifications of natural justice.
Matters of legal justice, then, are to the norms of
natural justice what the details of action are to practical norms in general. In this way the considerations
of legal justice are contained in moral science, which
treats of the basic premises.

---

[26] See above, p. 97.

[27] St. Thomas maintains that legal justice flows from
natural justice, not as a conclusion must follow from
principles (sicut conclusio ex principiis) but by way
of specification (per modum determinationis) (V,12,101-
118).

Again, when Thomas states that the primary and common principles of action are the same for all in regard to their correctness,[28] he is still speaking of a variable norm whose immutability is not that of a speculative universal. Since, then, there is an essential difference between practical norms and speculative truths, the primary principles are not the same for all agents in the precise way that speculative truth is the same for all spectators. The sameness for each agent is that of a variable norm, not that of a fixed truth.

Does the fact that there is a radical difference between the practical and speculative universal indicate that there is also a great difference between speculative and practical truth? If there is a great difference can one speak of the objectivity of moral truth in the same sense that one speaks of the objectivity of speculative truth?

To answer these questions, the first step is to note two texts of St. Thomas. In his commentary on the Ethics he says:

> To express the true and the false is an essential function of every intellect. But the good of the practical reason is not truth absolutely speaking but the conformable truth, i.e., truth corresponding to right desire. . . .[29]

In the Summa Thomas speaks in more detail of this distinction between the standards of speculative and practical reason:

> As stated in Ethic. vi.2, truth is not the same for the practical as for the speculative intellect. Because the truth of the speculative intellect depends on conformity between the intellect and the thing. And since the

---

[28] " . . . we must say that the natural law, as to general principles, is the same for all both as to rectitude and as to knowledge." S.T. I-II 94, 4c.

[29] " . . . dicere enim verum et falsum est opus pertinens ad quemlibet. Sed bonum practici intellectus non est veritas absoluta, sed veritas confesse se habens, id est concorditer, ad appetitum rectum . . . ." Sent. Ethic., VI,2,104-107.

intellect cannot be infallibly in conformity
with things in contingent matters, but only
in necessary matters, therefore no speculative
habit about contingent things is an intellectual virtue, but only such as is about necessary things. On the other hand, the truth
of the practical intellect depends on conformity with right appetite. This conformity
has no place in necessary matters, which are
not affected by the human will; but only in
contingent matters which can be effected by
us . . . .[30]

To explain these texts: the notion of truth implies
a relationship between the intellect and things. In the
case of absolute or speculative truth the intellect con-
forms to reality. For reality measures the intellect
and so is the standard to which the intellect must
conform.

But in the case of conformable or practical truth
the realities in question are ruled or measured by the
intellect. Now what is the standard or rule in the
light of which practical reason is said to have the
truth? This standard cannot be the deed enacted because the deed itself is measured. Nor can the standard
be reality because practical reason is concerning with
causing the realities in question. Consequently the
factor to which practical reason must conform must be
something within the agent himself. This factor according to St. Thomas is right desire.

There is then a great difference between speculative and practical truth because their standards differ.
Accordingly the universal norms of practical reason
cannot be objective in the way speculative universals
are. Practical universals are the flexible measures of
an indeterminate object, not the inflexible articulations
measured by a stable object. At the same time, one cannot call the norms of practical reason purely subjective
or merely relative or entirely situational. They are,
after all, norms which accord with right desire in regard to the goal and, therefore, have a kind of stability
which any universal must have. Nevertheless, this
stability is that of a flexible rule by which reason
measures and not that of a fixed truth by which reason
is measured.

---

[30] S.T. I-II,57,5,ad 3.

In moral philosophy, then, neither the terms "objective" nor "subjective" are adequate to expressing the notion of practical truth. This point should be kept in mind by those who reject purely relativistic or situational moral philosophies. Otherwise, one is in danger of overlooking an important distinction between speculative and practical truth. The most extreme example of such an oversight is that of Aristotle's opponents who, in looking for perfect certitude in matters of justice, concluded that there was no such thing as moral science. A less extreme example are those who, in making the object of moral philosophy the operable speculatively considered, are logically forced to regard practical truth in the same way as speculative truth. But to look at practical truth in this way is to unfit the moral philosopher for his basic task, which is to deal with the variables of action through the formulation of flexible norms.

The next question is: where is the standard of practical reason--right desire--to be found? In speculative science the standard is to be found in reality itself. Is the standard of practical reason to be found in the nature of things? After all, as was earlier shown,[31] legal justice is contrasted with natural justice in that the former is made by man but the latter is not. Or, perhaps, is the standard for the changeable norms of natural justice to be found in the unchangeable justice of the gods to which Aristotle referred earlier?[32] Or, finally, is the standard--right desire--to be found in the good man himself?

Since the answer to these questions depends upon a clear understanding of what is meant by right desire, the following text of Aquinas is pertinent.

> Desire is concerned both with the goal and
> with the means to the goal. The goal, how-
> ever, is determined for man by nature . . .
> while the means to the goal are not determined
> for us by nature but are found out through
> reason. Hence it is clear that right desire

---

[31]See above, p. 96, note 14.
[32]See above, p. 93.

in regard to the goal is the measure of
the truth of practical reason. Accordingly
the truth of practical reason is determined
in conformity with right desire. However
the truth of practical reason itself is the
right rule of desire in regard to the means
to the goal. . . .33

What is meant by the statement that man's goal is
determined for him by nature? Does it mean that the
goal is an actual entity existing apart from man as if
set there by nature? No. Here Thomas is referring to
a capacity for perfection which men may realize by
their operations.34

Now man has a natural but very general knowledge
of this goal and of the norms appropriate to its attainment. This knowledge of the precepts of the natural
law35 is the result of reason conforming to the fact
that man has a natural goal. Yet Thomas does not make
this goal but rather right desire the standard of
practical reason. Why? The answer is that for St.
Thomas practical reason is far more than reason simply
knowing the natural precepts. The knowledge of the
precepts is merely speculative as far as many men who
do not choose to live according to them are concerned.
And even if a man chooses to live according to these
precepts, his reason does not yet possess the practical
truth. He must first live by these precepts over a
great period of time in order to acquire virtue. Then
he has right desire, an habitual inclination to his

33"Et ideo dicendum est quod appetitus est finis et
eorum quae sunt ad finem; finis autem determinatus est
homini a natura. . ., ea autem quae sunt ad finem non
sunt nobis determinata a natura, sed per rationem in-
vestigantur; sic ergo manifestum est quod rectitudo appetitus per respectum ad finem est mensura veritatis in
ratione practica et secundum hoc determinatur veritas
rationis practicae secundum concordiam ad appetitum rectum, ipsa autem veritas rationis practicae est regula
rectitudinis appetitus circa ea quae sunt ad finem. . ."
(VI,2,114-125).

34See above, p. 73.

35" . . . in operativis sunt quaedam principia naturaliter cognita, quasi indemonstrabilia principia et pro-
pinqua his, ut malum esse vitandum, nulli esse iniuste

proper good. Only when right desire exists as an actual
operating principle does practical reason have the
standard which guarantees its possession of the practical
truth. As Thomas says above: "right desire in regard
to the goal is the measure of the truth of practical
reason. Accordingly the truth of practical reason is
determined in conformity with right desire."

Thomas goes on to say that, while the goal is
determined for man by nature, the means to the goal are
not determined for him by nature but are discovered
through reason. Here the contrast is between the goal
and the means to the goal and, therefore, between the
practical truth of universal norms and the practical
truth of particular judgments of choice. Now the
universal norms apply to all men. But particular judgments apply only to each particular man in his own
circumstances. Since the knowledge of the goal does not
include within it the knowledge of the means, the knowledge of the general norms does not include the knowledge
of the particular judgments about what is good in the
here and now. To use an oft repeated example, the norm
of courage is indeterminate as far as the acts of advancing or retreating in battle are concerned. From
the viewpoint of the norm alone, these acts are indifferent.[36] They do not include within their definition
a reference to man's goal and, therefore, cannot be
judged as either good or bad. But in the concrete there
is no such thing as an indifferent human act because
any actual deed either promotes or hinders man's attainment of his goal and so must be either good or bad.[37]

Consequently, each man must discover for himself
what he should choose. His practical reason, already
ruled by right desire in regard to the goal, itself

_____

nocendum . . ." <u>Sent</u>. <u>Ethic</u>., V,12,51-54.

[36]"But it may happen that the object of an action
does not include something pertaining to the order of
reason; for instance, to pick up a straw from the ground,
to walk in the fields, and the like: and such actions
are indifferent according to their species." <u>S.T</u>. I-II,
18, 8c.

[37]" . . . every human action that proceeds from de-
liberate reason, if it be considered in the individual,
must be good or bad." <u>S.T</u>. I-II, 18, 9c.

becomes the rule or standard for matters of choice. In
other words, the good man himself is the standard in
matters of choice.[38] In the light of his basic desires,
which supply an overriding direction to his life, he
looks over the variable world of his own circumstances
and picks out just the right means to satisfy his desire.
No one else can make this particular determination of
choice because no one else is he in his circumstances.
And no general norm determines this choice because norms
are indeterminate in this regard. When he chooses,
then, he is the sole judge and cause of a unique reality,
a good human act, which perfects him in the here and now.

In conclusion, the basic standard of practical
reason is to be found in the good man, who is the instance of right desire, the habitual inclination to
man's proper good. Because the good man is the instance
of this operating standard, he himself is the unique
standard in matters of choice. Consequently, the actions
of such men can provide the starting points for the inquiry of moral science. Since the individual acts of
virtue already contain the universal in the particular,
they may be studied in order to derive from them universal norms of action. The good man is already operating
with these guides in an experiential way. Nevertheless,
the articulation of this experience in universal terms
can be an aid to him.

So far there is nothing in the text to suggest that
there are natural standards of goodness which exist apart
from man like fully constituted entities which measure
his practical reason in the same way that reality measures
his speculative reason. But what happens when one introduces St. Thomas' notion of natural law? Thomas
does not mention natural law in his commentary on the
Ethics but does treat it extensively in the Summa
Theologiae.[39] Does this treatment contradict the conclusion that the good man is the standard of truth for
practical reason?

_____

[38]St. Thomas, commenting upon Aristotle, says: "Et
in hoc plurimum differt studiosus ab aliis quod in
singulis operabilibus videt quid vere sit bonum, quasi
existens regula et mensura omnium operabilium, quia
scilicet in eis iudicandum est aliquid bonum vel malum
secundum quod ei videtur" Sent. Ethic. III,10,88-91.

[39]S.T. I-II,91,2;94.

To answer that question it should be recalled that, while Aristotle and St. Thomas hold in common that the deeds of the good man provide the starting points for moral science, the good man varies with the cultural setting.[40] Consequently, the norms which Aristotle draws from the deeds of the good man are simply called natural. But the norms which St. Thomas draws from the deeds of the Christian are called precepts of the natural law. For the Christian sees himself as under the law of a personal creator who governs the universe according to a plan of reason called the eternal law.[41]

Now the fact that 1) there is an eternal law existing in God apart from man and that 2) there is an understanding of natural law existing in all men does not mean that a man necessarily possesses right desire. But only when right desire exists as a working principle on this earth does the moral philosopher have the actualities, good deeds, upon which he can base his reflections. These reflections give insight, not only into the precepts of the natural law, but more importantly into the norms of the virtues. Only with such insight can the philosopher understand what the eternal law is. Thus the philosopher defines the eternal law from what he knows in man. He does not define man from any direct knowledge of the eternal law.[42]

If one forgets that Thomas locates the standard of practical reason in right desire, he may be tempted to

---

[40]See above, p. 84.

[41]This plan comes under the analogous notion of law, which is defined as an ordinance of reason made by a ruler and promulgated to his subjects (S.T. I-II, 90, 4c). The promulgation of eternal law is the act by which God constitutes things in their own natures (Ibid., 91, 2c). Since non-rational creatures act according to their nature necessarily, they act according to natural law only in a broad sense. For law in a strict sense is given only to rational subjects. Thus, only man acts or does not act according to natural law (Ibid., 91,2, ad 3).

[42]Because the theologian takes the word of God as the first principle of his science, he may define man in terms of what God says about him.

think that moral science consists in deducing more
particular norms from the norms of the natural law.
The least that can be said about this moral geometry is
that it is certainly neither Aristotelian nor Thomistic
in inspiration.

II. The Demonstrative Method of Moral Philosophy

The next point to be shown is how the variable
object of moral science requires a method of reasoning
which is distinct from that of speculative science.
Along what general lines should the argument run in
order to establish this point?

To begin: scientific reasoning is about some
subject matter treated in universal terms in which one
progresses from premises to conclusions, from the known
to the unknown. The subject determines the type of
first premises which are induced from it, the manner of
moving from premises to conclusions, and the type of
conclusions reached. Consequently, if one wishes to
show the difference between the methods of speculative
and moral science, he must start by showing the differences in the subject.

The subject or object of speculative science is
any reality considered for the sake of the necessities
involved in it, while that of moral science is human
choices considered for the sake of choosing well. Consequently, the first premises induced from experience
of the way things are should be stable universals in
the case of speculative science. In the case of moral
science, the first premises induced from the experience
of acting should be flexible norms. The conclusions
drawn from the first premises (or principles) should
be stable universals about the causes of things in the
case of speculative science and particular judgments
about what should be done in the case of moral science.
The conclusions of moral science cannot be expressed in
universals because the truth about particular acts to
be done can be expressed only in particular judgments.
Finally, the method of reasoning from premises to conclusion must be analytic in speculative science because
one must reason from things, which are already known
as effects, to their causes, which are the necessities
involved in these things. In the case of moral science,
the reasoning must be synthetic because the basic premise
a flexible norm, must be applied as a kind of formal

cause to the details of action in order to see what effect should be produced.

Do the texts from St. Thomas' commentary verify the above outline of the argument? St. Thomas, commenting upon Aristotle, states:

> Because in the art of demonstrative science it is necessary that principles conform to conclusions, it is desirable and preferable when treating such subject-matter, that is, matter which is so variable, and when proceeding from such subject-matter, to manifest the truth in a rough way: that is, by applying universal and simple principles to the singular and the composite realm of action; for it is necessary in any practical science to proceed in a synthetic manner. In speculative science, on the contrary, it is necessary to proceed in an analytic manner by resolving the composite into its simple causes. . . .[43]

In the art of demonstrative sciences it is necessary that principles conform to conclusions. What are the principles and the conclusions of moral science? The basic principles are the starting points, the variable subject matter of human choices, from which (ex similibus) moral science draws its first premises.[44] The conclusions about which (de talibus) moral science is concerned are the variable matters of what should be chosen.

---

[43]"Et quia secundum artem demonstrativae scientiae oportet principia esse conformia conclusionibus, amabile est et optabile de talibus, id est tam variabilibus, tractatum facientes et ex similibus procedentes, ostendere veritatem primo quidem grosse, id est applicando universalia principia et simplicia ad singularia et composita in quibus est actus; necessarium est enim in qualibet operativa scientia ut procedatur modo compositivo, e contrario autem in scientia speculativa necesse est ut procedatur modo resolutivo, resolvendo composita in principia simplicia. . ." Sent. Ethic., I,3,47-58.

[44]The term "principle" may refer to any kind of starting point of some process. Thus the particular deeds from which the first premises are drawn are principles. So also is the first premise a principle

What must happen, then, if the principles are to
conform to the conclusions? Thomas answers that one
must "manifest the truth in a rough way." A little
later he says that one must show the truth "typically
or in outline."[45] And further on he notes that one
should speak "of what happens for the most part."[46]
In other words, the truth (the universal account) must
be presented broadly so that it may accommodate the
variable principles and conclusions of the argument.

In view of the fact that the truths of moral
science are to be expressed in broad or flexible premises
which can be used to reach conclusions about action, what
is the method of proceeding from the premises to the
conclusion? Aquinas describes it as "applying universal
and simple principles to the singular and composite realm
of action." The universal principles are the first norms
which are drawn by induction from one's experience of
human actions. As will be shown in a few moments, the
first universal of this type is that one should do good.
This principle is the most universal because all other
norms are simply more specific variations of it. It is
also the most simple because it is ultimate, i.e., no
other norm is prior to it. The method of reasoning,
then, is to apply this norm to the details of action
until the particular deed that should be done becomes
clear. In brief, one seeks what is to be done in the
light of first principles.

The above method of reasoning fits the description
of the practical syllogism.[47] The major premise is a

---

because it begins the scientific reasoning method.

[45] ". . . deinde oportet ostendere figuraliter, id
est verisimiliter, et hoc est procedere ex propriis
principiis huius scientiae, nam scientia moralis est de
actibus voluntariis, voluntatis autem motivum est non
solum bonum, sed apparens bonum . . ." Sent. Ethic.,
I, 3, 59-63.

[46] ". . . oportet ut, cum dicturi simus de his quae
ut frequentius accidunt, id est de actibus voluntariis,
quos voluntas non ex necessitate producit, sed forte in-
clinata magis ad unum quam ad aliud, ut etiam ex talibus
procedamus, ut principia sint conclusionibus conformia"
Sent. Ethic., I, 3, 64-69.

[47] St. Thomas, commenting upon Aristotle, describes
the practical syllogism as follows: ". . . una quidem

114

universal stating what good should be done or what evil avoided. The minor premise is a statement of fact about the particular that appears as good in the light of the major premise. And the conclusion is the particular judgment that the particular good should be done.

The above description of the practical syllogism may be adapted to the arguments of moral science in which all the premises are universals. As will be shown shortly, the movement of reason will be from more universal to more specific norms.

Since Thomas is describing the demonstrative method employed by Aristotle in the Ethics, this method is best illustrated by examining some of the arguments in that work. Aristotle, after a brief survey of the actions of men, the starting points of moral science, induces the truth that the highest good of man is happiness.[48] Further refelction shows that, while men agree on this point, they disagree about the precise nature of happiness. A survey of the actions of men shows that happiness may be divided into four general types.[49] The many think that happiness consists in the pursuit either of riches or of pleasure while the few think that it consists in the pursuit either of honor or of virtue.

The actions of men show such wide variations that the question naturally arises: what is real as opposed to apparent happiness? In order to answer this question, one must settle on the most universal and simple norm which is to be accepted as the ultimate guide to action. Since the fact of man having a proper good, happiness, has already been induced from experience, and since it is the very nature of man's proper good that it should be chosen, it follows that the first principle is that

---

universalis, puta: 'Omne inhonestum est fugiendum'; alia autem est singularis circa ea quae proprie per sensum cognoscuntur, puta: 'Hic actus est inhonestus.' Cum autem ex his duabus opinionibus fiat una ratio, necesse est quod sequatur conclusio . . . Sent. Ethic., VII,3, 234-239.

[48]E.N. I,4,1095a19.
[49]E.N. I,5,1095b13-17.

man should choose good.[50] What must happen now is that this universal be applied to the various choices of men in order to demonstrate which of these choices is the most proper.

Aristotle proceeds with the demonstration in an informal way in Chapter Five of Book One and in a more formal way in Chapter Seven. The argument may be summarized as follows. Happiness has the nature of the highest or final good because it alone is sought for its own sake while all other goods are sought for its sake. Consequently, the universal principle that man should do good must be applied to all the actions of men to see which constitutes man's real good. In the light of this principle the good man clearly sees that neither riches nor pleasure nor honor constitutes man's proper good. Although men as a matter of fact lead their lives in the pursuit of these goods as if they were man's highest good, the prudent man does not. Instead, he chooses to lead his life in the pursuit of virtue, choosing all other goods for its sake. The conclusion of the first demonstration, then, is that man should choose to pursue virtue. The major is that all men should choose their proper good. The minor is that the pursuit of virtue is man's proper good. And the conclusion is that all men should choose the pursuit of virtue.

In this demonstration all of the propositions are universals. Yet the demonstration is also practical because it results from applying a universal to the details of action in order to discover a more specific norm of action. This process of demonstration continues throughout the whole of the Ethics[51] and concludes with

---

[50]St. Thomas holds that the universal norms of action follow upon the intellectual apprehension of what is good. "Consequently the first principle in the practical reason is one founded on the notion of good, viz., that good is that which all things seek after. Hence this is the first precept of law, that good is to be done and pursued, and evil is to be avoided." S.T. I-II 94, 2c.

[51]For texts that illustrate how Aristotle, after concluding one part of the argument with a statement which is still merely an outline of the truth, proceeds to fill in the details of the outline by continuing the

the proof that all men should choose to pursue the good of contemplation.[52] This norm in turn is applied to the details of political life, a process which takes place in the Politics.[53] The result of this whole demonstrative process is a specific norm which must then be applied by each prudent man to the details of his life. One may say, then, that the universal demonstrations of moral science build up the major premise of a strictly practical syllogism, which is then applied to the details of action by the prudent man.

The actual practice of Aristotle, then, illustrates what St. Thomas maintains is the demonstrative method of moral science. Because the starting point from which the inquiry of moral science proceeds is the variable choices or actions of men, the universal drawn from them must be a flexible outline of the truth. Because the conclusions to which moral science proceeds are the variable matters of what man should choose, the universal guides to these actions must be outlines of the truth. And because the moral philosopher considers universal norms primarily for the sake of action, the demonstration starts with the most universal norm, proceeds on through more specific norms, and culminates in the particular actions of the prudent man.

St. Thomas concludes that text above (p.113) by contrasting the synthetic method of moral science, which he has just outlined, with the method of speculative science, which he describes as "to proceed in an analytic manner by resolving the composite into its simple causes . . . " The terms "synthetic" and "analytic" have a range of meaning which extends beyond the methods of the sciences.[54] The intention of the

---

argument, see the following: I,7,1098a2021; II,1,1103b26-30; II,7,1107a27-31; VI,1,1138b25-35. These texts amply justify the view of St. Thomas that practical demonstrations are synthetic in nature.

[52]E.N. X,7,1177a11-1178a8.

[53]See X,9,1179a33-1179b4 where Aristotle, explaining that the conclusions reached in the Ethics are still only outlines of the truth, argues that the inquiry must proceed on into the Politics.

[54]For a conprehensive study of these terms, see Edmund Dolan, F.S.C., "Resolution and Composition in

coming discussion, however, is to examine how these terms
apply to three areas in order to distinguish them from
the method of moral science. These areas are speculative science, mathematics and deliberation.

An analytic inquiry begins with things which are
first as far as man's understanding is concerned but
last in the nature of things. It concludes with things
which are last in man's understanding but first in the
nature of things.[55] How is this general method of inquiry applicable to the methods of metaphysics and
natural philosophy? The starting points of these sciences are sensible things which, since they are particular and composite, are what is first known by man.
These realities, however, are secondary in the nature of
things because they are composite effects which depend
for their existence upon causes, which are simple.
Consequently the composites must be analyzed or resolved
into their basic causes or elements until the truth
about the causes is discovered. In these sciences, then,
one reasons from effect to cause.

Human actions may also provide the material for an
analytic inquiry, a point that was shown in the earlier
examination of Aristotle's introductory argument.[56]

St. Thomas holds that the inquiry of deliberation
(counsel) is also analytic.

> Now the principle in the inquiry of counsel
> is the end, which precedes indeed in inten-
> tion, but comes afterwards into execution.
> Hence the inquiry of counsel must needs be
> one of analysis, beginning that is to say,
> from that which is intended in the future,
> and continuing until it arrives at that

Speculative and Practical Discourse," Laval theologique
et philosophic, 6, (1950), 9-62.

[55] " . . . if that which precedes in knowledge is
later in the order of being, the process is one of
analysis, as when our judgment deals with effects,
which by analysis we trace to their simple causes."
S.T. I-II, 14, 5c.

[56] See above, pp. 66-67.

which is to be done at once.[57]

Here the movement is from effect to cause, the end being the intended effect and the cause being the act of choice. When the agent chooses to act on the last step of his analysis, he initiates a series of acts which will result in the attainment of the end.

On the other hand, a synthetic inquiry has for its starting point that which is first in regard to man's knowledge and also first in regard to status in reality. Reason then proceeds to what is secondary both in regards to knowledge and in regards to reality.[58]

How is the method of this inquiry applicable to the method of mathematics? Aquinas notes that "if the same thing is more knowable to us and more knowable absolutely, reason proceeds from principles, as in mathematics."[59] In geometry, for example, the figure is primary in regard to man's knowledge because it is known by abstraction from sensible imagination. The figure is also primary in the nature of things because it is a formal cause of all the properties or effects which flow necessarily from it. Thus the reasoning of geometry is from cause to effect.

How is the synthetic method applicable to the sphere of action? As was previously noted, the deliberative inquiry preceding action is from effect to cause, the analytic method characteristic of speculative science. Here one is not yet in the realm of action. One enters this realm only after the agent, seeing that the means are available, chooses to act. Without this act of choice, there is no realm of action. As soon as this realm is entered, the movement is synthetic. If the project is of some complexity, one act follows another

---

[57]S.T. I-II, 14, 5c.

[58]"In every inquiry one must begin from some principle And if this principle precedes both in knowledge and in being, the process is not analytic, but synthetic: because to proceed from cause to effect is to proceed synthetically, since causes are more simple than effects." S.T. I-II, 14, 5c.

[59]" . . . si quidem eadem sint nobis magis nota et simpliciter, tunc ratio procedit a principiis, sicut in mathematicis . . . " Sent. Ethic., I,4,125-126.

in a series until the final effect, a composition, is attained. Builders compose materials to build a house. Good men put together acts to create a truly human order

Despite similarities there is an important difference between the synthetic patterns of geometry and of action. In geometry one can examine the figure, the formal cause, and deduce the properties or effects flowing necessarily from it. In action, however, one cannot simply examine the formal cause, a universal norm, and deduce the effects that must flow from it. For the universal norm includes the effect, the particular deed, only in an indeterminate way. The agent himself must step in and determine the effect in the light of his particular circumstances. This reasoning from cause to effect, then, is not strictly deductive.

Now Thomas describes the method of moral science as synthetic.[60] Because this method is concerned with action, it is not deductive like that of geometry. Because this method is from cause to effect, it is not deliberative. And because this method is of an intellectual construct, it is distinct from actual operations What then is the synthetic method of moral science? The method flows from what moral science is. And moral science is an intellectual aid developed by the good man, who is already engaged in constructing a human order. In fashioning this aid, the good man takes the most universal norm of action, a formal cause, and applies it in successive stages to the actions of life. The more specific norms that emerge from this application are those of the moral virtues, which perfect man's lower nature. The next norms to emerge are those of the intellectual virtues, particularly the virtue of contemplation, which perfects man's higher nature. The

---

[60]For a contrary opinion, see the article of Edmund Dolan previously cited in note 54, p. 117. Dolan asks: "Must we now conclude that not only counsel but also formally practical science proceeds resolutively (analytically) in the same way that demonstrative science proceeds resolutively?" (p.50). Later he answers: "Although practical discourse cannot be denominated resolutive in the particular sense that characterizes demonstration propter quid, still it participates the common notion of resolution" (p.58).

final result is a norm precisely stating man's highest good, reflecting the steps that have been already taken to attain this good and prefiguring the steps that should be taken to project the human order into the future. The final norm, then, is the result of an intellectual composing which is to serve as the guide for actually composing a good society.

The foregoing account does not pretend to exhaust the complexities involved in the question of the method of moral science. It does attempt, however, to show that St. Thomas' precise statements about questions of method are quite coherent. This coherence has been achieved by concentrating on the act of choice, from which moral science derives its norms and for which that science is designed as an aid. If one loses sight of the centrality of the act of choice, he is apt to be confused by the many texts of Thomas on analysis and synthesis, on the speculative and the practical. He may find himself in a jungle of comparisons, contrasts and analogies in which everything seems to be either like or unlike everything else, depending on one's viewpoint. To extricate himself from the maze, he may attempt to catalogue all of the pertinent texts. But the danger of such an approach is to overemphasize words and ideas. The philosophy of St. Thomas, however, derives its inspiration from things in the speculative order and choice in the practical order. One then judges the word or idea against the reality and not the other way around. Consequently, any thinker must try to look at the realities themselves and judge both his own and the ideas of St. Thomas in their light. Now the thesis of this book is that there is indeed a radical distinction between the objects of speculative and practical science stemming from the fact that choice is central to the practical endeavor. Applying this view to the texts primarily of the commentary, we do seem to have a key to the maze. At any rate the discussion of the moral philosophy of St. Thomas would seem to be advanced if the question of the radical distinction were taken up and examined by others. Whatever the outcome, the discussion would at least be on a central point.

III. The Qualifications of the Student of Moral Philosophy

What qualifications must a man have if he is to understand and use the demonstrations employed by the

teacher of moral philosophy? The basic qualification
is that the student must already be a virtuous man.

The texts in this section are quite clear on this
point and so do not require any elaborate analysis. In
fact, if this book were written, not to settle a problem,
but simply to present an introduction to the notion of
moral science, it would have started with an examination
of these texts. They present a clear picture of the
virtuous man, from whose actions the articulations of
moral science are derived and for whose purposes these
articulations are shaped. Consequently, the reader
would have before him from the beginning a clear idea
of the source from which moral science develops.

Since, however, this study has been concerned with
the solution to problems about the nature of moral
science, it had to adopt a scientific mode of exposition.
In other words, it had to go back to the root of the
problem by discussing the object of moral science.
Thus the discussion about the learner is left to the
end just as Aristotle and St. Thomas leave it to the
end in their presentation.

If the texts are so clear, why have their meaning
apparently been missed by the commentators? One possible explanation is that, if one assumes that moral
science is speculative either entirely or to some degree, he will assume that even a bad man may acquire
this knowledge. He will grant, of course, that if this
knowledge is to be used well, the learner must be a
good man. Thus he may easily read the texts as supporting this notion. But he will not make the very acquisition of the knowledge of practical science dependent
upon the learner being a prudent man. For, he will
argue, cannot even an imprudent sinner be an expert in
moral science. At any rate, what do the texts say?

St. Thomas, commenting upon Aristotle, states that
the student:

> should accept whatever is said to him by
> another in the same way, i.e., in the manner
> that suits the material, because it is
> characteristic of the learned or well
> instructed man to seek as much certitude
> in any matter as its nature allows. For
> there cannot be as much certitude in
> variable and contingent matters as in

122

necessary matters which are always the
same. Therefore the educated man neither
requires more certitude nor is content with
less than suits the thing which he treats.[61]

The learner should have enough intellectual training to appreciate the difference between the types of
certitude characteristic of speculative and practical
demonstrations. There are, however, further qualifications of a less intellectual nature which are needed
by the student. Thomas, commenting upon Aristotle,
notes:

> No one can be a good student unless he
> has some knowledge of what he should study.
> But the young do not have knowledge of the
> things belonging to moral science, which
> are mostly known by experience. A young
> man is inexperienced in the operations of
> human life because of his lack of years.
> Nevertheless, the explanations of moral
> science proceed from and are about the
> actions of human life.[62]

---

[61]"Et dicit quod debitum est quod unusquisque reci-
piat unumquodque eorum quae sibi ab alio dicentur eodem
modo, id est secundum quod convenit materiae, quia ad
hominem disciplinatum, id est bene instructum, pertinet
ut tantum certitudinem quaerat in unaquaque materia
quantum natura rei patitur; non enim potest esse tanta
certitudo in materia variabili et contingenti sicut in
materia necessaria semper eodem modo se habente, et ideo
auditor bene disciplinatur nec debet maiorem certitudinem
requirere nec minori esse contentus quam sit conveniens
rei de qua agitur" Sent. Ethic., I,3,72-84.

[62]". . . oportet quod nullus sit auditor conveniens
nisi habeat aliquam notitiam eorum quae debet audire;
sed iuvenis non habet notitiam eorum quae pertinent ad
scientiam moralem, quae maxime cognoscuntur per experientiam, iuvenis autem est inexpertus operationum humanae
vitae propter temporis brevitatem et tamen rationes
moralis scientiae procedunt ex his quae pertinent ad
actus humanae vitae et etiam sunt de his . . ." Sent.
Ethic., I,3,116-124.

Because the purpose of moral science is to derive norms from facts already known so that the norms can be used as guides to the actions of life, the young cannot be good students because they do not have experience of the facts. They simply have not lived long enough to play a significant role in the affairs of men and so learn about themselves and others in the process. Students without this experience are like young engineers who have not yet built anything. They may possess some theoretical knowledge but this knowledge is about as much use to them as lectures on how to play the piano are of use to those who have not tried to play the piano.

Length of years, however, cannot be the only requirement. The fact that a man is old does not necessarily mean that he possesses the experience from which moral science is drawn. St. Thomas, commenting upon Aristotle, says:

> Thus it makes no difference whether men are
> prevented from being students of this science
> either by youthfulness in age or youthfulness
> in character, i.e., a follower of his
> passions, because, as the youthful in age
> fail to achieve the goal of this science
> that is knowledge, so the youthful in character
> fail to achieve the goal that is action.[63]

The young in character—those who follow their passions either on principle or out of weakness—are unqualified insofar as the goal of this science is action. One may well argue, however, that they fail even insofar as the goal is knowledge, which is not simply that of the most general norms but of a detailed account of all the virtues. The man of vice, who may consider the courageous man to be a fool, is not likely to accept the general norms. And the weak man, while accepting the general norms, is not likely to understand or appreciate them in detail. For the norms of the virtues are derived from the experience of the virtuous

---

[63]"Et sic nihil differt quantum ad hoc quod arceantur ab auditu huius scientiae iuvenis aetate vel iuvenis moribus, scilicet passionum sector, quia, sicut iuvenis aetate deficit a fine huius scientiae qui est cognitio, ita ille qui est iuvenis moribus deficit a fine qui est actio . . ." Sent. Ethic., I,3,150-155.

man. Hence one must be virtuous in order to understand
and appreciate the good man's account of the virtues.
Thus the man who lacks virtue fails even in attaining
the goal of knowledge.

So far, it is clear that the student of moral
science should be a prudent man. But how does he become prudent? The answer is that he must have had long
practice in trying to act according to reason so as to
eventually acquire harmony between reason and passion.
But how does he know what to practice? Does he follow
the general principles naturally known by all men until
he develops a good character? While this suggestion is
true enough, it may be misleading. Man does not come
into the world as if he were a new Adam, a kind of
purely natural man who precedes all culture and builds
up his character alone by acting according to his natural
lights. Man is born into families and communities
which already have a definite character, either good,
bad or middling. Consequently, the laws and customs
of a community make all the difference in the world as
far as the individual's perception of good is concerned.

St. Thomas, commenting upon Aristotle, expresses
the intimate connection between virtue and custom as
follows:

> . . . moral virtue arises from habit, i.e.,
> from customary practice. For moral virtue
> is in the appetitive part, from which there
> comes a certain inclination to desirable
> things. This inclination comes either from
> nature, which inclines to that which is
> suitable to it, or from custom, which turns
> into nature. Hence the word for moral
> virtue is taken from the word for customs
> . . . .[64]

---

[64]"Sed moralis virtus fit ex more, id est consuetudine. Virtus enim moralis est in parte appetitiva, unde
importat quandam inclinationem in aliquid appetibile,
quae quidem inclinatio vel est a natura quae inclinat
in id quod est sibi conveniens, vel ex consuetudine quae
vertitur in naturam. Et inde est quod nomen virtutis
moralis sumitur a consuetudine. . ." Sent. Ethic., II,1,
56-64.

For the individual, moral virtue arises from
continual efforts to bring the passions in line with
reason so that what the agent feels to be a good is
actually a good. Thus man's natural capacity or inclination to his proper good is strengthened by an inclination that comes from habit, which operates as a kind
of second or perfecting nature. For the community,
sound customs and laws arise from a history of collec-
tive choices which promote the community's attainment
of its natural good. These customs articulate what
the community loves and hates, enjoys and abhors. They
have their power over men, not primarily by argument,
but by what the community praises and blames, rewards
and punishes. Thus an imprint is put upon the emotional
life of the young long before they reach the full
status of adults. Without this kind of training it is
hard to imagine how individuals can attain the experience
needed by the student of moral philosophy.

The texts above show quite clearly that the student
of moral science must be virtuous because the goal of
this science is the knowledge of the practical truth
for the sake of action. Only the good man can meet
these goals of action and of knowledge. Concerning
the goal of action, only he has the capacity to act
well[65] and, therefore, the ability to use norms in the
proper way.

Concerning the goal of knowledge, only the good
man is equipped to know consistently what is right in
the particular. He is the immediate norm or standard
of choice. In such matters he has a kind of sight or
perception[66] which comes to him in his experience of

---

[65]It should be remembered that a good act is a
perfect response of a man--heart, mind and will--to the
situations in which he finds himself. Thus just as fine
paintings come from skilled artists or extraordinary
feats come from great athletes, so excellent deeds come
from men of excellence.

[66]The text of St. Thomas supporting this and the
rest of the statements in the paragraph is as follows:
"Quia enim dictum est supra quod intellectus qui est
principiorum operabilium consequitur experientiam et
perficitur per prudentiam, inde est quod oportet attend-
ere his quae opinantur et enuntiant circa operabilia
homines experti et senes et prudentes, quamvis non

126

life much as good judgment about matters of art or music comes to the trained artist or musician. The good man has a certitude about the truth of particulars which is analogous to that of the speculative thinker about his first principles. Thus the basic knowledge that moral science seeks is already found in its fundamentals in the good man, who acquires them, not primarily by argument, but through the experience of himself and his elders. A man can be prudent, then, without having acquired the intellectual virtue of moral science.

If, however, a good man seeks the aid of universal practical reason, he has but to reflect upon his experience of particular acts of temperance, courage, justice, prudence and contemplation in order to formulate practical norms of action. Since the particular contains the universal, he already has the facts or starting points or principles of moral science.[67]

Because the commentators hold that the object of moral science is some form of the operable speculatively considered, they quite logically conclude that the character of the knower is an incidental factor in the acquisition of this science. For if a science is speculative, the character of the spectator is an incidental factor in his acquisition of the truth. Thus both John of St. Thomas and Maritain maintain that one can be an expert in moral science and yet be an imprudent sinner. Quite clearly, then, these thinkers locate the first principles of moral science, not in the prudent man himself, but in the objective nature of things.

One consequence of placing the first principles of moral science in the objective nature of things is that

---

inducant demonstrationes, non minus quam ipsis demonstrationibus, sed etiam magis. Huiusmodi enim homines, propter hoc quod habent ex experientia visum, id est rectum iudicium de operabilibus,vident principia operabilium; principia autem sunt certiora conclusionibus demonstrationem" Sent. Ethic., VI,9,228-239.

[67]"Quia oportet in moralibus accipere ut principium quia ita est, quod quidem accipitur per experientiam et consuetudinem, puta quod concupiscentiae per abstinentiam superantur" Sent. Ethic., I,4,141-144.

the discussions of the moral philosopher will be too
speculative and so actually work against the practical
aims of the agent.[68] For example, if human choice is
considered simply for the sake of truth, the inquirer
must argue for its existence and nature with all the
thoroughness and rigor proper to a speculative treatment. Such a discussion is out of place in a practical
moral science because the existence of choice constitutes
a first principle of this study. What good man has a
practical doubt about whether he can choose or not? And
who strives to formulate general norms for the attainment
of some goal without assuming that man can choose al-
ternative ways of acting? When the nature of choice is
discussed, it is discussed in a manner suitable to the
requirements of a practical science. And when the
knowledge acquired in the speculative sciences is used,
it is used to meet a practical, not a speculative goal.
In brief, if moral philosophy is not seen as growing
from the experience of the good man, that science will
be inadequate to his needs.

---

[68]The difference between speculative and practical
argument is well expressed by Aristotle in his discussion of the difference between matters of argument and
of perception. "Not every problem, nor every thesis,
should be examined, but only one which might puzzle one
of those who need argument, not punishment or perception.
For people who are puzzled to know whether one ought to
honor the gods and love one's parents or not need punishment, while those who are puzzled to know whether snow
is white or not need perception" (Topics I,11,105a2-7).
In speculative inquiry it is certainly a matter of
argument whether the gods exist or not. But in a practical inquiry the existence of the gods is taken for
granted as a matter of proper upbringing. If such
matters or moral perception are denied, the remedy is
punishment and not argument. It makes a great deal of
difference, then, whether a question is treated speculatively or practically. For the starting points of
argument are quite different from those of practice.

CHAPTER VI

CONCLUSION

St. Thomas maintains that moral philosophy is scientific without being speculative and practical without being identical with prudence. In brief, moral philosophy is a scientific instrument which flows from and is used by the prudent man. Accordingly, moral philosophy occupies a definite place between speculative science on the one hand and the virtue of prudence on the other. The notion of a moral science, then, is quite complex. And this complexity accounts for the difficulties of the commentators.

John of St. Thomas assumes that if a study is scientific, it must be speculative. Consequently, he overlooks the explicit statement in the commentary of St. Thomas on the _Ethics_ that moral philosophy is a practical science employing the synthetic method.[1] Instead he bases his views on the text from the _Summa_ which speaks of the operable speculatively considered as occupying a middle position between the non-operable speculatively considered and the operable practically considered.[2] By making the middle category the object of moral science, he places this science between the speculative sciences on the one hand and prudence on the other. But this scheme bears only a superficial resemblance to that of St. Thomas. For in making moral science essentially speculative in nature, John of St. Thomas endangers the independent status of moral science by making it ultimately reducible to speculative science. The outcome, then, is a scheme in which there is only speculative science on the one hand and prudence on the other. In effect, the notion of practical science has been eliminated.

The commentators following John of St. Thomas are placed under a double burden. They must deal not only with the inherent difficulty of the notion of a practical science but also with the influence exerted by a respected predecessor. The commentator who comes

---

[1] See above, p. 23, note 52.

[2] See above, pp. 20-21.

closest to lifting this burden is Maritain. As was shown before,[3] Maritain, while he is reluctant to disagree with John of St. Thomas, maintains that moral philosophy as traditionally conceived is speculatively practical rather than simply speculative. Judging that such a science is not adequate to meet the needs of the practical man, Maritain introduces into the tradition the notion of a practically practical moral science which requires that its possessor also be a prudent man. According to Maritain, then, the middle category between speculative science on the one hand and prudence on the other is occupied by a moral science which is twofold in nature. There is the speculatively practical and the practically practical. While this proposal of Maritain is not in accord with St. Thomas, it has the merit of calling attention to the Thomistic view that there is an intimate connection between moral science and prudence.

Lottin, however, rejects Maritain's addition of a practically practical moral science to the traditional notion of moral philosophy. He maintains that, between speculative science on the one hand and prudence on the other, there is a moral philosophy which is both speculative and practical. Here Lottin seems to be more sensitive to the novelty of Maritain's proposal rather than to the problem in the tradition with which Maritain is wrestling.

This brief review of the opinions of the commentators shows why the commentators have not been successful in fully grasping St. Thomas' notion of moral philosophy. However there is one writer, Joseph Owens,[4] who has opened the way for a fresh look at the problem. He has focused his attention mainly on the notion of moral science as explained by Aristotle himself in the Nicomachean Ethics. In this way the difficulties inherent in the notion of a study which is both scientific and practical are squarely faced. Consequently, acquaintance with the work of this writer is a tremendous

---

[3]See above, p. 26, note 58.

[4]His works on this subject are listed in the bibliography.

help to one investigating the commentary of St. Thomas on the _Ethics_.

What is the view of St. Thomas? His view is that human choice may be considered either speculatively or practically. When considered simply for the sake of truth, human choices are contingent entities considered for the sake of the necessities involved in them. Thus they constitute a conceptually stabilized object to which the spectator's reason must conform in order to possess the objective truth. The method of this study is analytic, as is the method of any study which considers contingent effects in the light of their causes. Furthermore, this study is part of speculative science. Finally, the prudence of the spectator is an incidental factor in this consideration of human choice.

When, however, human choice is considered practically, Aquinas maintains it to be the object of moral philosophy. Here the agent considers the variables of human action for the sake of choosing well, a variable goal. To construct an intellectual aid for dealing with this variable object, the agent generalizes his own experience in order to formulate flexible norms which are to be applied to the realm of particular actions. This process requires that the agent be a prudent man. The universal norms, then, derive their validity from conformity, not to the way things are, but to right desire. And they derive their effectiveness from the fact that the prudent man, reasoning synthetically from cause to effect, accommodates flexible norms to the variable circumstances of his own life. Finally, moral science in the practical realm is neither subordinate to nor part of speculative science. It uses the truths of speculative science, but in its own way for its own purposes.

Since the views of the commentators bear more resemblance to a speculative than to a practical consideration of human choice, there still remains the task for Thomistic thinkers to construct a moral philosophy along the general lines laid down by St. Thomas. While this science should conform to the principles of Aquinas to be considered Thomistic, it must by the same token be suitable to the times. For the essence of a practical inquiry according to the conception of Aquinas is that its formulations arise from and be applied to particular choices. But particular choices only exist in particular cultures.

Consequently, just as the ancients constructed a moral science to deal with the problems of a Greek city state or of a medieval kingdom, so the modern man must work his moral science out from start to finish in the arena of contemporary life. A moral philosophy which does not proceed in this way cannot be according to the conception of St. Thomas.

BIBLIOGRAPHY

Adler, Mortimer. "Aristotle's Conception of Practical Truth and the Consequences of that Conception." Paideia. Second Special Issue. 1978, pp. 158-166.

Aquinas, St. Thomas. Aristotle's De Anima. Tr. K. Foster et al. New Haven: Yale University Press, 1951.

_____. Commentary on Aristotle's Physics. Tr. Blackwell et al. London: Routledge & Kegan Paul, 1963.

_____. Commentary on the Metaphysics of Aristotle, Tr. John Rowan. Chicago: Henry Regnery Co., 1961.

_____. Commentary on the Nicomachean Ethics. Tr. C. I. Litzinger. 2 vols. Chicago: Henry Regnery Co., 1964.

_____. The Disputed Questions of Truth. Tr. Robert W. Mulligan et al. S.J. 3 vols. Chicago: Henry Regnery Co., 1952.

_____. The Division and Methods of the Sciences. Tr. Armand Maurer. 3rd ed. Toronto: The Pontifical Institute of Mediaeval Studies, 1963.

_____. De Sensu et Sensato. 3rd ed. Ed. Spiazzi. Taurini: Marietti, 1973.

_____. Expositio Super Librum Boethii de Trinitate. Ed. Bruno Decker. Leiden: E. J. Brill, 1955.

_____. Physicorum Aristotelis. Ed. Maggiolo. Taurini: Marietti, 1965.

_____. Questiones Disputatae. In Opera Omnia. Leonine Edition. Ed. A. Dondaine. Vol. 22, Pt. I, Q. 1-7. Romae: Ad Sanctae Sabinae, 1970.

_____. Scriptum super IV libros Sententiarum. Ed. Mandonnet-Moos, (4 vols.), Paris: 1929-1947.

_____. Sententia Libri Ethicorum. In Opera Omnia. Leonine Edition. Ed. R. A. Gauthier. Vols. 47½ and 47. Romae: S. C. de Propaganda Fide, 1969.

133

_____. _Summa Theologiae_. 4 vols. Ottawa: Studii Generalis O. Pr., 1941.

Aristotle. _The Works of Aristotle_. Ed. W.D. Ross. 2 vols. Chicago: Encyclopedia Britannica, Inc., 1952.

Bourke, Vernon. _Ethics_. N.Y.: Macmillan, 1951.

_____. "The Nicomachean Ethics and St. Thomas Aquinas." _Commemorative Studies: St. Thomas Aquinas 1274-1974_. Toronto: Pontifical Institute of Mediaeval Studies, 1974, pp. 239-259.

_____. "The Role of a Proposed Practical Intellectual Virtue of Wisdom." _Proc. of the Amer. Cath. Philos. Assoc._, 26 (1952), 160-167.

Caietanus, Thomas de Vio, Card. Commentaria in _Summam totius Theologiae Santi Thomae Aquinatis_. Omnia opera iussa edita Leonis XIII P.M. Romae: 1882-1930.

Caldera, Rafael-Tomas. _Le jugement par inclination chez Saint Thomas D'Aquin_. Paris: J. Vrin, 1980.

Chapman, Emmanuel. "Relation of _Ethics_ and _Politics_." _Proc. of the Amer. Cath. Philos. Assoc._, 15 (1939), 176-180.

Cornford, Francis MacDonald. _The Republic of Plato_. Oxford: Oxford University Press, 1945.

Deman, Th. "Sur l'organisation du savoir moral." _Revue des Sciences philos. et theol._, 23 (1931), 268.

Dolan, Edmund, F.S.C. "Resolution and Composition in Speculative and Practical Discourse." _Laval Theologique et philosophique_, 6 (1950), 9-62.

Eschmann, Ignatius, T. "St. Thomas's Approach to Moral Philosophy." _Proc. of the Amer. Cath. Philos. Assoc._, 31 (1957), 25-33.

Fagothy, Austin. _Right and Reason_. St. Louis: The C.V. Mosly Co., 1959.

Gredt, J. _Elementa Philosophiae Aristotelico-Thomistica_ Herder: Friburgi Bresgoviae, 1937, 6th Ed.

Grisez, Germain G. "The Logic of Moral Judgment." Proc. of the Amer. Cath. Philos. Assoc., 36 (1962), 67-76.

Hardie, W. F. R. Aristotle's Ethical Theory. Oxford: Clarendon Press, 1968.

Jaffa, Harry V. Thomism and Aristotelianism: A Study of the Commentary on the Nicomachean Ethics. Chicago, 1952.

Joachim, H. H. Aristotle: The Nicomachean Ethics. Ed. P. A. Rees. Oxford: Clarendon Press, 1951.

John of St. Thomas. Cursus Philosophicus Thomisticus. Ed. B. Reiser. Vol. I. Ars Logica. Turin: Marietti, 1930.

_____. The Material Logic of John of St. Thomas. Tr. Yves Simon et al. Chicago: University of Chicago Press, 1955.

Lottin, Odon. Morale Fondamentale. Vol. I. Tournai: Desclee, 1954.

_____. Principes de Morale. Vol. I. Louvain: Editions de l'Abbaye du Mont Cesar, 1946.

Marietan, Joseph. Probleme de la classification des sciences d'Aristote a s. Thomas. Paris: 1901.

Maritain, Jacques. The Degrees of Knowledge. Tr. G. B. Phelan et al. New York: Scribner's, 1959.

_____. Moral Philosophy. Ed. Joseph W. Evans. New York: Charles Scribner's Sons, 1964.

_____. Neuf lecons sur les notions premieres de la philosophie morale. Paris: Alsatia, 1953.

_____. Science and Wisdom. New York: Scribner's, 1940.

May, William E. "The Structure and Argument of the Nicomachean Ethics." The New Scholasticism, 36 (1962), 1-18.

Mullaney, James V. "The Natural Terrestial End of Man." The Thomist, 18 (1955), 373-395.

McGovern, Thomas. "Ethics as a Science." Proc. of the Amer. Cath. Philos. Assoc., 36 (1962), 59-66.

McInerny, Ralph M. "Ethics and Subjectivity." Proc. of the Amer. Cath. Philos. Assoc., 36 (1962), 111-118.

_____. "The Degrees of Practical Knowledge." Conference - Seminar on Jacques Maritain's The Degrees of Knowledge. St. Louis: The American Maritain Assoc., 1981, 119-135.

_____. "Ethics and Verification." Wisdom in Depth: Essays in Honor of Henri Renard. S.J. Ed. by V. F. Daues, M. R. Holloway, L. Sweeney. Milwaukee: Bruce, 1966, pp. 157-173.

Naus, John. The Nature of the Practical Intellect According to St. Thomas Aquinas. Rome, Gregoriana, 1959.

Oesterle, John A. Ethics. Englewood Cliffs, N.J.: Prentice-Hall Inc., 1957.

_____. "Theoretical and Practical Knowledge," The Thomist 21 (1958), 146-161.

Owens, Joseph. "Aquinas as Aristotelian Commentator." Commemorative Studies: St. Thomas Aquinas 1274-1974. Toronto: Pontifical Institute of Mediaeval Studies, 1974, pp. 213-238.

_____. "Aristotelian Ethics, Medicine, and the Changing Nature of Man." Philosophical Medical Ethics: Its Nature and Significance. Ed. S. Specker and H. T. Englehardt, Jr. Boston: D. Reidel Publishing Co., 1977, pp. 127-142.

_____. The Doctrine of Being in the Aristotelian Metaphysics. 2nd ed. Toronto: Pontifical Institute of Mediaeval Studies, 1963.

_____. "The Ethical Universal in Aristotle." Studia Moralia, III. Rome, 1965, 27-47.

_____. "The Grounds of Ethical Universality in Aristotle." Man and World, 2 (1969), 171-193.

_____. "Nature and Ethical Norm in Aristotle." Akten. XIV Intern. Kongr. Philos., V, 442-447.

_____. "Value and Metaphysics." Future of Metaphysics. Ed. Robert E. Wood. Chicago: Quadrangle Press, 1970, pp. 204-228.

Petrin, Jean, O.M.I. Connaissance speculative et connaissance pratique. Ottawa: Editions de L'Universite Ottawa, 1948.

Ramirez, J.M. "La science morale pratique." Bulletin thomiste, 4 (1934-36), 425.

Renard, Henri, S.J. The Philosophy of Morality. Milwaukee: Bruce Publishing Co., 1953.

Simon, Yves. Critique de la connaissance morale. Paris: Desclee, de Brouwer et cie, 1934.

_____. "Introduction to the Study of Practical Wisdom." The New Scholasticism, 35 (1961), 1-40.

Stewart, J.A. Notes on the Nicomachean Ethics of Aristotle. 2 vols. Oxford: Clarendon Press, 1892.

Sullivan, Roger J. Morality and the Good Life: A Commentary on Aristotle's Nicomachean Ethics. Memphis: Memphis State University Press, 1977.

Wallace, William. The Role of Demonstration in Moral Theology. Washington, D.C., The Thomist Press, 1962.

William, Sister Mary. "The Relationship of the Intellectual Virtue of Science and Moral Virtues." The New Scholasticism, 36 (1962), 475-505.

INDEX